高职高专旅游英语系列教材

Extensive Reading for Tourism English

旅游英语泛读

主 编 戴丽萍 郝立英

副主编 李 辉

清华大学出版社

北京交通大学出版社

·北京·

内 容 简 介

本书共 8 个单元，每个单元包括 3 篇文章（长度控制在 800～1 000 个单词），每篇文章均配有相关的练习。Think Before Reading 模块旨在培养学生的阅读预测能力。作为重要阅读技巧之一，在仔细阅读之前通过标题、段首句等预测文章大意对理解文章大有裨益。练习模块（选择题、搭配题、判断题、简答题和填空题是本书的主体练习模式）提供了词汇层面和篇章层面的各种阅读训练，并将阅读技巧训练融入每项阅读任务当中，使学生在关注"读到了什么"的同时学会"怎么读"，强化了阅读效果。

本书可作为高职高专院校旅游英语及相关专业的教材使用，也可作为旅游从业者或旅游爱好者的自学教材和读物。

图书在版编目（CIP）数据

旅游英语泛读 / 戴丽萍，郝立英主编. — 北京 ： 北京交通大学出版社 ：清华大学出版社，2020.6
　ISBN 978-7-5121-3961-9

　Ⅰ. ① 旅…　Ⅱ. ① 戴…　② 郝…　Ⅲ. ① 旅游–英语–阅读教学–高等学校–教材
Ⅳ. ① F59

中国版本图书馆 CIP 数据核字（2019）第 151975 号

旅游英语泛读
LÜYOU YINGYU FANDU

责任编辑：	张利军
出版发行：	清华大学出版社　　邮编：100084　　电话：010-62776969　　http://www.tup.com.cn
	北京交通大学出版社　邮编：100044　　电话：010-51686414　　http://www.bjtup.com.cn
印 刷 者：	北京时代华都印刷有限公司
经　　销：	全国新华书店
开　　本：	185 mm×230 mm　　印张：7.75　　字数：175 千字
版 印 次：	2020 年 6 月第 1 版　　2020 年 6 月第 1 次印刷
印　　数：	1～3 000 册　　定价：36.00 元

本书如有质量问题，请向北京交通大学出版社质监组反映。对您的意见和批评，我们表示欢迎和感谢。
投诉电话：010-51686043，51686008；传真：010-62225406；E-mail：press@bjtu.edu.cn。

"高职高专旅游英语系列教材"编委会

王建荣　　任　淼　　李　辉　　李家坤

张志华　　陈琳琳　　林　昊　　周　迎

周红红　　赵　挺　　郝立英　　戴丽萍

阎　莉　　张雅娜

前言
Preface

改革开放 40 多年来，我国取得了举世瞩目的伟大成就，发生了翻天覆地的变化，而旅游业也以其强劲的势头成为我国经济发展中最具活力的"朝阳产业"。随着改革开放的不断深化，我国的旅游业正面临着前所未有的跨越式发展机遇。无论是国内旅游，还是跨境旅游，其规模越来越大，品种越来越多，层次越来越高，旅游业已从单纯的游玩上升为一种文化性产业。因此，旅游业的不断发展对旅游从业人员的素质要求也越来越高。他们不仅需要丰富的专业知识，而且随着跨境旅游规模的不断扩大，过硬的英语交流能力已成为他们提升竞争力的主要技能。为尽快培养出合格的旅游从业人才，满足旅游市场的需要，促进我国旅游事业的蓬勃发展，编写一套系统而实用的旅游英语教材是十分必要和紧迫的。

为满足我国高职高专院校旅游英语专业教学的迫切需求，适应当前我国旅游业的快速发展，我们组织国内部分高校从事旅游英语教学的骨干教师编写了这套"高职高专旅游英语系列教材"。本系列教材主要包括《旅游英语口语》《旅游英语会话》《旅游英语听力（第 1 册）》《旅游英语听力（第 2 册）》《旅游英语泛读》5 本教材。

本系列教材具有以下特点。

（1）以任务为导向，以交际为主旨。本系列教材配有大量的练习，学练一体，课文内容和练习与现场操作实务密切相关，学生完全能够学以致用，学习效率高。学生不仅可以与其他同学互练，也可以进行自主练习，大量操练语言输出。

（2）选材贴近专业，取材真实广泛。本系列教材的选材均来自地道的旅游方面的原版文章和会话，材料真实，贴近专业，融知识性、真实性和趣味性于一体，学生学起来有兴趣、有动力、效率高。

（3）教材设计科学，互补性强。本系列教材根据高职高专学生的特点设置教学内容，每个单元的学习量适中，简练易学。本系列教材基本涵盖了旅游英语的听、说、读、写功能，能够体现旅游特色和交际功能，从基础口语、专业会话、词汇扩充和专业知识阅读等方面进行了系统的内容安排，使学生能够大幅提升旅游英语综合应用能力。

（4）在娱乐中学习，以兴趣促提高。本系列教材除了在每个单元安排大量实用性强的学习内容之外，还选用了许多能够激发学生学习兴趣的音频和视频资料，如歌曲、语言故事、著名景点介绍和图片等，让学生在娱乐中汲取专业知识，巩固专业基础。

本书为《旅游英语泛读》，共 8 个单元，是为"旅游英语泛读"课程编写的教材。

本书的每个单元包括 3 篇文章，每篇文章的长度控制在 800～1 000 个单词，而且每篇文章均配有相关的练习。"Think Before Reading"模块旨在培养学生的阅读预测能力。作为重要阅读技巧之一，在仔细阅读之前通过标题、段首句等预测文章大意对理解文章大有裨益。练习模块（选择题、搭配题、判断题、简答题和填空题是本书的主体练习模式）提供了词汇层面和篇章层面的各种阅读训练，并将阅读技巧训练融入每项阅读任务当中，使学生在关注"读到了什么"的同时学会"怎么读"，强化了阅读效果。

为了方便课堂教学和学生自主学习，本书配有学习指导、视频讲解、模拟试题、练习答案等教学资源。学习指导不仅可以指导学生如何进行学习，还就教材的学习内容进行辅导，具体包括学习重点及学习难点、学习目标及学习要求、预备知识、学习课时安排、学习内容及指导、语言归纳及常见错误分析、知识扩展等，是学生自主学习和教师课堂教学不可或缺的辅助材料。视频讲解是对教材内容的精讲，旨在为学生提供更好的自主学习资源和学习途径。模拟试题紧密结合教材内容编写而成，在题型设计上充分考虑对学生旅游英语阅读理解能力的考查，涉及语言材料广泛，贴近实际工作和生活。练习答案则针对教材中的练习题及模拟试题提供相应的解答。读者可先扫描书后的防盗码获取资源读取权限，然后再扫描书中每单元开始处的二维码来获取相应的教学资源。

本书的主要特色如下。

（1）内容新颖，时代感强。本书在选材上注重信息性、可思性和前瞻性，题材广泛，内容丰富，主要涉及语言、文化、习俗等方面。

（2）知识性与趣味性并重。本书结合高职高专学生的特点，从学生的学习兴趣和关注的焦点出发，做到语言活泼、生动，让学生在学习旅游英语的过程中获得乐趣。

（3）实用性强。本书的练习形式（如正误判断、多项选择、简短回答等）兼顾学生旅游英语应用能力的提升。选材和练习设计重视词汇的反复操练和知识面的扩大，有助于学生快速熟悉旅游业务知识，提高旅游英语水平。

（4）配备立体化的教学资源，通过文本及音频、视频、动画等多种媒体形式来呈现教学内容，为学生提供可资学习的旅游英语阅读材料，帮助学生提高阅读能力，同时也方便学生自主学习。

在本书构思、选材、编写、审稿和出版过程中，众多学者和一线工作人员给我们提出了宝贵的意见和建议，同时也得到编者所在院校及出版社的大力支持。在此，全体编写人员向他们致以诚挚的谢意。

由于编写时间仓促且编写人员水平有限，书中疏漏之处在所难免，欢迎广大读者批评指正。

编　者
2020 年 5 月

目录

Contents

Unit 1

Customs and Festivals

Festivals are an expressive way to celebrate glorious heritage (文化遗产), culture and traditions. They are meant to rejoice (欢庆) special moments and emotions in our lives with our loved ones. They play an important role in adding structure to our social lives, and connect us with our families and backgrounds. They give us a distraction (娱乐) from our day to day, exhausting routine of life, and give us some inspiration to remember the important things and moments in life. Festivals were started to pass the legends, knowledge and traditions onto the next generation.

Passage I

Easter

Think Before Reading

1. Do you know the origin of Easter?
2. Do you know the story of *the Last Supper*?
3. What are the traditional activities on Easter?

Easter is a Christian holiday that celebrates the belief in the resurrection (复活) of Jesus Christ from the dead. In the New Testament of the Bible (《新约圣经》), the event is said to have

occurred three days after Jesus was crucified (钉死在十字架上) by the Romans and died in roughly 30 A.D. Easter falls on a different date each year, but always on a Sunday between March 22nd and April 25th. The holiday concludes the "Passion of Christ," a series of events and holidays that begins with Lent (四旬斋) — a 40-day period of fasting (斋戒), prayer and sacrifice (祭祀) — and ends with Holy Week (圣周), which includes Holy Thursday [the celebration of Jesus' Last Supper with his 12 Apostles (门徒)], Good Friday (on which Jesus' death is observed), and Easter Sunday.

According to the New Testament, Jesus was arrested by the Roman authorities, essentially because he claimed to be the "Son of God," although historians question this motive, with some saying that the Romans may have viewed him as a threat to the empire. He was sentenced to death by crucifixion, and the subsequent resurrection three days later proved that he was the living son of God. The resurrection of Jesus is essentially the foundation upon which the Christian religions are built. Hence, Easter is a very significant date on the Christian calendar.

Despite its significance as a Christian holy day, many of the traditions and symbols that play a key role in Easter observances (庆祝) actually have roots in pagan (异教徒) celebrations and in the Jewish holiday of Passover (逾越节). Notably, Easter is associated with the Jewish holiday of Passover. These links are clearly seen in the Last Supper, which occurred the night before Jesus' arrest and the sufferings Jesus endured following

his arrest. The Last Supper was essentially a Passover feast. However, the New Testament describes it as being given new significance by Jesus: He identified the matzah (or bread) he shared with his 12 apostles as his "body" and the cup of wine they drank as his "blood". These rituals (仪式) would come to symbolize the sacrifice he was about to make in death, and became the basis for the Christian ritual of Holy Communion, which remains a fundamental part of Christian religious services.

There are many Easter-time traditions with roots that can be traced to non-Christian and even pagan or non-religious celebrations. Many non-Christians choose to observe these traditions while essentially ignoring the religious aspects of the celebration. Examples of non-religious Easter traditions include Easter eggs, and related games such as egg rolling and egg decorating. It's believed that eggs represented fertility (生育能力) and birth. Egg decorating may have become part of the Easter celebration <u>in a nod to</u> the religious significance of Easter, i.e., Jesus' resurrection or re-birth. Many people — mostly children — also participate in Easter egg "hunts", in which decorated eggs are hidden.

In some households, a character known as the Easter Bunny delivers candy and chocolate eggs

to children on Easter Sunday morning. These candies often arrive in an Easter basket. The exact origins of the Easter Bunny tradition are unknown, although some historians believe it arrived in America with German immigrants in the 1700s. Rabbits are, in many cultures, known as enthusiastic procreators (繁殖者), so the arrival of baby bunnies in springtime meadows became associated with birth and renewal.

An Easter dinner of lamb also has historical roots, since a lamb was often used as a sacrificial animal in Jewish traditions, and lamb is frequently served during Passover. The phrase "lamb of God" is sometimes used to refer to Jesus and the sacrificial nature of his death.

Today, Easter is a commercial event as well as a religious holiday, marked by high sales for greeting cards, candies (such as Peeps, chocolate eggs and chocolate Easter bunnies) and other gifts.

I. Choose the best choice to answer or finish each of the following questions.

1. Which of the following days does NOT belong to Holy Week?

   A. Holy Thursday.　　　B. Good Friday.　　　C. Easter Sunday.　　　D. Lent.

2. What makes Easter become a very important festival on Christian calendar?

   A. The holiday begins with Lent and ends with Holy Week.

   B. The resurrection of Jesus proves that he is the living son of God.

   C. The Christian religions are built on the foundation of the resurrection of Jesus.

   D. Easter is associated with the Jewish holiday of Passover.

3. What is the ritual of Holy Communion according to the passage?

   A. People share bread and wine.

   B. People have a Passover feast.

   C. People offer sacrifices to God.

   D. People sing praise songs to God.

4. Which of the following statements is true according to the passage?

   A. The phrase "lamb of God" is used to refer to an Easter dinner.

   B. The tradition of egg rolling has nothing to do with religious significance of Easter.

   C. The character of Easter Bunny originated from pagan celebrations.

   D. The religious aspects of the Easter celebration are ignored by many non-Christians.

5. What's the meaning of "in a nod to" in Paragraph 4?

   A. In order to show agreement.

   B. In order to express respect and admiration.

   C. In order to show understanding.

   D. In order to give someone a sign to do something.

II. Match the words with their definitions.

WORDS	DEFINITIONS
1. motive	A. express indirectly by an image, form, or model
2. religion	B. to bring something to an end
3. symbolize	C. a particular system of belief in a god or gods
4. conclude	D. a principle, an idea or a fact that something is based on
5. foundation	E. a reason for doing something

III. Please name at least three traditional activities of Easter.

1. _____.

2. _____.

3. _____.

 **Passage II**

Customs of the Spring Festival

Think Before Reading

1. What is the superstition in sweeping while doing the house cleaning? What should people do?

2. Why is there a custom of burning crackers on the Spring Festival?

Chinese New Year or Spring Festival is the most important of the traditional Chinese holidays. It is sometimes called the Lunar New Year, especially by people outside China. The festival traditionally begins on the first day of the first lunar month in the Chinese calendar and ends on the 15th; this day is called Lantern Festival. The Spring Festival is the most important festival for the Chinese people and is when all family members get together, just like Christmas in the West. All people living away from home go back. Many customs accompany the Spring

Festival. Some are still followed today.

House Cleaning

The entire house should be cleaned before Chinese New Year's Day. On New Year's Eve, all brooms (扫帚), brushes, dusters, dust pans and other cleaning equipment are put away. Sweeping or dusting should not be done on Chinese New Year's Day for fear that good fortune will be swept away. After Chinese New Year's Day, the floors may be swept. Beginning at the door, the dust and rubbish are swept to the middle of the parlor (客厅), then placed in the corners and not taken or thrown out until the fifth day. At no time should the rubbish in the corners be trampled (踏，踩) upon. In sweeping, there is a superstition (迷信) that if you sweep the dirt out over the front entrance, you will sweep one of the family away. Also, to sweep the dust and dirt out of your house by the front entrance is to sweep away the good fortune of the family; it must always be swept inwards and then carried out, then no harm will follow. All dirt and rubbish must be taken out the back door.

Reunion Dinner

A reunion dinner is held on Chinese New Year's Eve where members of the family, near and far away, get together for the celebration. The venue (地点) will usually be in or near the home of the most senior member of the family. The New Year's Eve dinner is very sumptuous (丰盛的) and traditionally includes chicken and fish. In some areas, fish is included, but not eaten completely (and the remainder is stored overnight), as the Chinese phrase "may there be surpluses (盈余) every year" sounds the same as "may there be fish every year."

Red Packets

Traditionally, red envelopes or red packets are passed out during the Chinese New Year's celebrations, from married couples or the elderly to unmarried juniors. It is also common for adults or young couples to give red

packets to children. Red packets are also known as Ya Sui Qian, literally, the money used to suppress (镇压) or put down the evil spirit during this period.

Red packets almost always contain money, usually varying from a couple of dollars to several hundred. Per custom, the amount of money in the red packets should be of even numbers, as odd numbers are associated with cash given during funerals (葬礼). One exception is the number four as it is considered bad luck, because the word for four is a homophone (同音字) for death, money in red envelopes never adds up to $4. However, the number 8 is considered lucky (for its homophone for "wealth"), and $8 is commonly found in the red envelopes. Sometimes chocolate coins are found in the red packets.

Burning Crackers

Burning crackers was once the most typical custom on the Spring Festival. People thought the spluttering (噼啪作响) sound could help drive away evil spirits. However, such an activity was completely or partially forbidden in big cities once the government took security, noise and air pollution factors into consideration. As a replacement, some buy tapes with firecracker sounds to  listen to, some break little balloons to get the sound too, while others buy firecracker handicrafts to hang in the living room.

Everyone, young and old, rich and poor, looks forward to celebrating the noisiest, most joyous and longest festival of the year. For Chinese at home and abroad, the Spring Festival is always the most important festival.

I. Match the words with their definitions.

WORDS	DEFINITIONS
1. transportation	A. coming together again
2. reunion	B. a custom or belief that has existed for a long time
3. joyous	C. taking people or goods from one place to another
4. tradition	D. a special enjoyable event
5. celebration	E. extremely happy

II. Decide whether the following statements are true or false according to Passage II.

1. The Spring Festival in China is as important as Christmas in the West. (   )

2. The floors should be swept from the door to the middle of the parlor on New Year's Day. (   )

3. In a reunion dinner, fish will not be eaten completely. (   )

4. During the Chinese New Year, children may get the red packets with $4 in them. (   )

5. The custom of burning crackers is still very popular in big cities nowadays. (   )

III. Fill in the blanks in following passage with words from Passage II.

Chinese New Year or Spring Festival is the most important 1_____ festival for the Chinese people and just like Christmas in the West. Some customs accompanying the Spring Festival are still followed today. House cleaning should be done before, but not on New Year's Day in case good 2_____ will be swept away. A 3_____ dinner is held on Chinese New Year's Eve where members of the family will get together. Red packets, also known as Ya Sui Qian, are passed out from 4_____ to children. The amount of money in the red packets should be of even numbers except four. Burning crackers which was once the most 5_____ custom, is forbidden in some big cities for the sake of environment.

Passage III

The Mid-Autumn Festival

Think Before Reading

1. Do you know the origin of the Mid-Autumn Festival?
2. Can you tell some legends about the moon?
3. What are the traditional activities on the Mid-Autumn Festival?

The traditional Mid-Autumn Festival enjoys great popularity in China where it is second only to the Spring Festival, or Chinese New Year, and in some of its neighboring countries.

The Mid-Autumn Festival falls on the 15th day of the eighth lunar month. Since ancient times, people have celebrated it by worshipping and admiring the glorious full moon, and enjoying osmanthus (桂花) flowers and fermented-osmanthus wine (发酵桂花酒). The Chinese believe that the full moon represents family reunions. Therefore, the Mid-Autumn Festival is also a day for families to get together and for those far away from home to think of their loved ones.

Influenced by the Chinese culture, certain other countries in East and Southeast Asia also celebrate the Mid-Autumn Festival. In 2006, the holiday was added to the list of China's first batch of national intangible cultural heritages (非物质文化遗产).

Origins

The Mid-Autumn Day, as the name suggests, usually falls in late September. As the full moon implies family reunions, it is also called the "reunion festival".

The Chinese people's tradition of worshiping the moon and offering sacrifices to it can be traced back more than 2,000 years. The Mid-Autumn Festival also happens to be a harvest season.

To show their gratitude to Heaven for a good harvest, the Chinese ancients held celebratory (庆祝的) activities around this day. At this time of year, it's cool, but not yet cold. Clear skies and crisp (清新的) air make it a good time to enjoy the beauty of the full moon. Hence, later, celebrations of the festival laid greater emphasis on enjoying the moon rather than making sacrifices, as new connotations (含义) became attached to it.

Ancient customs, rites (仪式), myths (神话), legends (传说) and other factors of traditional Chinese cultures have combined to imbue (赋予) the Mid-Autumn Festival with rich content and

cultural connotations in its evolution (演变). The most famous legends told around the festival are fairy tales about the Moon Palace, relating to such figures as the Moon Goddess, and Tang Dynasty Emperor Li Longji (685–762) and his concubine (妃子) Yang Yuhuan.

In the seventh century, the Mid-Autumn became an established festival as related celebrations of a bright full moon and feasting (盛宴) became prevalent. In the 10th century, the mooncake, a special dessert for the day, made an appearance, and the festival became even more popular as the accompanying celebrations evolved. By the 14th century, its importance was second only to that of the Spring Festival.

Customs

Offering Sacrifice to the Moon

The sacrifice to the moon on the Mid-Autumn Festival has a very long history, which dates back to the Zhou Dynasty (1046–256 BC). In ancient times, the emperors usually offered a sacrifice (献祭) to the moon on the Autumnal Equinox (秋分) at the place called Altar of the Moon (月坛). The Altar of the Moon in Beijing was where the emperors of the Ming (1368–1644) and Qing (1644–1911) Dynasties offered a sacrifice to the moon. Through the passage of time, this custom has been adopted into folklore (民间传说) and now the sacrificial ceremony (祭祀仪式) is usually held in family units. However, nowadays this activity continues only in certain rural areas or at attraction sites and no longer by the majority of

Chinese families. At the Mid-Autumn Festival, a memorial tablet (牌位) to the Moon Goddess is set up in each household with fruits, melons and mooncakes placed in front of it as a sacrifice. The cake must be round and melons and fruits cut into lotus-petal-shaped (莲花瓣状的) pieces.

The offerings would be set on a table that the moonlight could reach, or facing the general direction of the moon on cloudy or rainy nights. In front of the table was an incense burner (香炉), with lighted red candles on each side. Some people also buy joss paper (纸钱) with images of the Goddess and patterns like the Jade Rabbit making heavenly medicine printed on it. After the moon-worshipping ceremony, people burn the joss paper and family members share the fruits and moon cakes. At the

festival of family reunion, people give each other mooncakes as gifts to express their good wishes.

Appreciating the Moon

Compared with the moon sacrificial ceremony, the custom of appreciating the moon is much more popular among modern people. The family members sit around a table and appreciate the moon, while talking to each other and eating the offerings from the ceremony, etc. The custom was actually derived from (源于) the sacrificial ceremony, which made a serious activity into a relaxing one. It started in the Three Kingdoms Period (220–280 AD) to the Jin Dynasty (265–420 AD). In the Tang Dynasty (618–907 AD), the custom became very popular. There are many works of literature of that time praising the moon and expressing yearnings (思念) to distant relatives and friends. It was during the Song Dynasty (960–1279 AD) that a folk festival involving appreciation of the moon was formed and it became the earliest official Mid-Autumn Festival.

Eating Moon Cakes

The origin is attributed to the victorious insurrectionary (起义者) army of the Yuan Dynasty (1271–1368 AD) that had passed messages by hiding notes in moon cakes. As gifts, the leader gave moon cakes to his subordinates (属下) on the coming Mid-Autumn Festival. Since then, the custom of eating moon cakes on Mid-Autumn Day became established. In the following eras, after the moon sacrificial ceremony, the official (官员) cut the biggest moon cake into even pieces based on the number of family members and passed them around to each of them. Even those who could not make it home on the night had a piece reserved for them because the moon cake signified (象征) reunion and the cake sacrificed to the moon was considered auspicious (吉祥的). Nowadays, although most families do not hold the sacrificial ceremony, family members still gather together to share the delicious round moon cakes on the festival night.

Other Customs

In addition to these common customs, there are those that are popular in certain areas on Mid-Autumn Day. In southern China, children play with festival lanterns. In Hong Kong, one of the most important activities is the fire dragon dances; in Shanghai, people go out for moon

appreciation instead of staying inside and they burn incense buckets (香桶). In Taiwan, people set off sky lanterns and single girls steal vegetables, which hopefully can bring them a "Mr. Right". These form only the tip of the iceberg (冰山一角). Although originally a festival among the Han Chinese, the Mid-Autumn Festival is now very popular among ethnic minorities (少数民族) too and they have some unique and interesting customs, such as chasing the moon of Mongolians (蒙古族人), seeking the moon of Tibetans (藏族人) and dancing in the moonlight of the Yi people, etc. If one attends a Mid-Autumn Festival in China, they will find more interesting customs for sure.

I. Choose the best choice to answer or finish each of the following questions.

1. A full moon represents _____ in Chinese culture.

   A. love   B. family reunions   C. romance   D. harvest

2. When did the moon cake appear in China?

   A. In the Three Kingdoms Period.   B. In the Tang Dynasty.

   C. In the 7th century.   D. In the 10th century.

3. The offerings would NOT be set _____.

   A. in an incense burner   B. in front of the memorial tablet

   C. on a table that the moonlight could reach   D. on a table facing the general direction of the moon

4. The custom of appreciating the moon was derived from _____.

A. the transformation of sacrificial ceremony from a serious activity into a relaxing one

B. the activities of praising the moon and expressing yearnings

C. the gifts exchange after the moon-worshipping ceremony

D. the worship of the Moon Palace and the Moon Goddess

5. What's the unique custom of Mongolians in the Mid-Autumn Festival?

A. Dancing in the moonlight.   B. Chasing the moon.

C. Seeking the moon.   D. Setting off sky lanterns.

II. Match the words with their definitions.

WORDS	DEFINITIONS
1. lunar	A. be common at a particular time or in a particular place
2. reunion	B. to recognize the good qualities of sb./sth.
3. prevalent	C. be relating to the moon
4. appreciate	D. having a very pleasant taste or smell
5. delicious	E. the act of people coming together after they have been apart for some time

III. Decide whether the following statements are true or false according to Passage III.

1. Some countries in East and Southeast Asia also celebrate the Mid-Autumn Festival. ( )

2. Celebrations of the Mid-Autumn Festival laid emphasis on making sacrifices. ( )

3. Offering sacrifice to the moon is still popular among the majority of Chinese families nowadays. ( )

4. The moon cakes being used in the sacrificial ceremony must be round. ( )

5. The custom of appreciating the moon was involved in the Mid-Autumn Festival during the Song Dynasty. ( )

6. The origin of the moon cake is relevant to the victorious insurrectionary army. ( )

7. The moon cake was considered auspicious after being sacrificed to the moon. ( )

8. There are different customs in different areas on Mid-Autumn Day. ( )

9. The fire dragon dance is one of the most important activities in Taiwan. ( )

10. The ethnic minorities in China do not celebrate the Mid-Autumn Festival. ( )

Unit 2

Cultural Differences

Lead-in

Communication can prove much more complex (复杂) than many realize. This is especially true within a cross-cultural society. Cultural differences in communication are influenced by many factors, such as language barriers (障碍), nonverbal (非语言) communication, and a lot of culturally common expressions often used inside of one culture but not translatable within another. All of these factors often combine creating a great deal of misunderstanding.

Passage I

How to Use Good Communication Skills for Cross-Cultural Diversity (多样化)

Think Before Reading

1. Have you had any experiences of communicating with people from different cultures?
2. Did you experience any misunderstandings with people from other countries?
3. Do you know any special skills for communications across different cultures?

The business environment of the 21st century is expanding (扩大，扩展) to include people from cultures and countries around the world. It takes special skills to communicate across these many cultures. Your courtesy（礼节）and respect help build a good foundation for good communication. People respond to courtesy and feel comfortable when they know they have your respect. This helps them to be open and willing to ask questions when they don't understand something. By making people feel comfortable, you help them to be better listeners.

Slow down when you speak. Allow those who don't have the same native language as you the time to interpret what you are saying.

Speak clearly and concisely. Make eye contact and express clearly. Avoid using ambiguous (有两种或多种意思的) words. One of the problems non-native-English-speaking cultures have with the English language is misunderstanding the many meanings one word can have.

Keep it simple. Think in terms of your audience, and speak to their understanding. Don't make long speeches that lose your group. Allow listeners the time to think about what you have said. Pay attention to your audience and be an active speaker and listener. You can be sure that the

group has understood your communication by their response to your words.

Show respect and courtesy to people who come from different cultures. When you respect the people you communicate with, this helps reduce the stress they feel when trying to understand what you are saying. Doing basic research on specific ways to interact with the cultures you will be coming into contact with is a great way to show your multi-cultural group that you respect them.

Smile and be open. Your body language communicates your acceptance (接受) — or non-acceptance — and respect, as it helps put listeners at ease. Your body language conveys (传达) unspoken communication. Avoid large gestures with your hands, as this can be intimidating (威胁) to people who might misunderstand your meaning. Keeping your arms crossed often makes people think you are not open to what they have to say.

Avoid slang (俚语). Slang words are unique (仅有的) to individual cultures and not always interpreted correctly. To ensure good cross-cultural communication, don't use slang words others might not know.

Avoid humor. What is funny in one culture might not be in another. Humor might be misunderstood and interpreted in a bad light. While humor is a good icebreaker, it can backfire when the cross-cultural group misses humor's meaning. When in doubt, avoid using humor when communicating with people from many cultures.

Adopt a formal communication approach (方法) until you develop a good relation with your group. An informal approach can be upsetting to people from different cultures, especially when you have just met them. Use a respectful and formal way of speech until you have developed a relationship with your cross-cultural group.

Stay away from using negative (否定) questions or answers. Double negatives are confusing enough to those with English as their native language. In a cross-cultural situation, double negatives are easily misunderstood. Keep questions and answers simple so everyone understands.

Ask for feedback (反馈). Request members of the cross-cultural group to speak up and provide interaction or ask questions. This helps prevent misunderstandings and clears up questions people might have.

Summarize what you have said. Don't assume (假定) that just because you said it everyone understands. Repeat what you have said in a different way, summarize it and allow people the time to grasp what you have said. By summarizing what you have said, you can be sure that everyone is on the same page.

I. Choose the best choice to answer or finish each of the following questions.

1. In the passage, the author aims to _____ .

   A. tell us that cross-cultural communication is very difficult

   B. show us some useful methods for cross-cultural communication

   C. show us the big differences between different cultures

   D. tell us humor is very important in cross-cultural communication

2. According to the author, when you allow those who don't have the same native language as you the time to interpret what you are saying, the word "interpret" means "_____".

   A. translate into one's native language

   B. explain to others

   C. make clear the meaning of

   D. summarize

3. From this passage, we can learn how to _____ .

   A. show the diversity of cultures

   B. explain the importance of cultural differences

   C. use some useful skills of communication across cultures

   D. use double negatives in cross cultural communication

4. Which of the following statements is true according to the passage?

   A. Humor can help people understand each other in cross cultural communication.

   B. You should use formal method before you are very familiar with the audience.

   C. Feedback is not necessary because it may lead to misunderstanding.

   D. People can learn faster if you use as many slang words as possible.

5. When the author says "everyone is on the same page", he means everyone _____ .

   A. gets confused in the same way

   B. is reading the same page of the textbook

   C. looks at the same blackboard

   D. is faced with the same situation

II. Match the words with their definitions.

WORDS	DEFINITIONS
1. respond	A. act on each other
2. interact	B. take an idea or custom
3. summarize	C. act in answer to
4. adopt	D. understand with the mind
5. grasp	E. give the main points only

III. Please name at least six approaches to make people comfortable in cross-cultural communication.

1. _____.
2. _____.
3. _____.
4. _____.
5. _____.
6. _____.

Good Job? Cultural Communication Differences

Think Before Reading

1. When an American says "You have done a good job" to you, do you believe he really means it ?
2. Why do Americans often say "Thank you" when you have done something you should do?

I was surprised a few months ago when a Pakistani (巴基斯坦人) in one of my workshops asked me, "Do Americans mean it when they say: 'Good job'?" My instinct (本能) was to say，"Sure. What makes you think they don't?" But then I realized the answer was more complicated, and it actually gets down to a key difference between American and other work environments.

What I finally ended up telling the man was this, "They mean it in the sense that they really appreciate it when people do something for them, even if it's the person's job, but it's also not very important because they say it all the time and to pretty much everyone. In short, don't get too excited when your manager says "Good job." "Thank you," he said, "because that did not come through in my recent performance evaluation."

I realized the man had interpreted "good job" as fairly strong praise when in fact it was just the American's way of expressing appreciation. To put it another way, in cultures where managers do not often thank employees just for doing their jobs, positive feedback (反馈) of any kind is unusual and perhaps quite significant, meaning a very favorable performance evaluation and maybe even a promotion.

This was actually not the first time I have met with this cultural difference. Europeans often become annoyed with the amount of positive feedback Americans give. They feel that you are given a salary for doing your job and to be praised for that is almost to suggest your manager was not expecting you to do your job. I have actually heard the same point made by Americans, in the other direction, "European managers don't appreciate us; they never tell us we're doing a good job." To which a European would probably reply, "Of course not. We don't treat our employees like children."

So what's going on here? In particular, what accounts for the

American tendency (倾向) to thank people for doing their job? To be honest, I'm not completely sure. I've thought about this for some time, and the best explanation I have found for this behavior

is somehow related to the deep egalitarian streak (平等主义倾向) in American culture. For example, a core American belief is that no one is better than anyone else, whether by birth, social class, education, or wealth.

Americans do not believe all people are the same — far from it — but they strongly believe that everyone is equal. Some people are wealthier, smarter, better-educated, and better-looking than others, but at the end of day even the president of the United States is not better than a bellman or a maid (女仆). Indeed, one recent president of the United States, Jimmy Carter, went to great pains to make exactly that point when he was shown on national TV carrying his own suitcase into the White House after a weekend trip to Georgia. The message was unmistakable: I may be president of the United States, but I can carry my suitcase into my house just like everyone else does. It's noteworthy in this context (环境) how candidates (候选人) for president always stress their humble roots.

The point is that if we are all equal, then no one owes anybody else anything; we may choose to do things for other people, but we are under no obligation (义务). Even in the workplace no one can force us to do our job; the most they can do is fire us if we don't. But the choice is ours.

How else to explain why we thank the plumber (管道工) who fixes our pipes, the waiters and waitresses who serve us our food? We're paying these people, for heaven's sake! I think we thank them because we want them to know that we know they did not have to help us.

Back in the workplace when we say "good job" or when we thank someone for doing what we pay them to do, in some sense we're simply acknowledging (承认) that everyone has a choice in these matters. And it's just good manners to express appreciation. And that's the point — it's just being polite, but it's not really praise. But if you come from a culture where expressions of this kind of appreciation are uncommon, like my Pakistani friend, you can be easily misled and get the wrong idea about your job performance.

So if you're a non-American on the receiving end of "good job", don't read too much into it. And if you're an American handing out "good job" right and left, you may be giving your non-American staff the wrong impression.

I. Match the words with their definitions.

WORDS	DEFINITIONS
1. appreciate	A. difficult to do or understand
2. complicated	B. effect produced on the mind or feelings
3. significant	C. low in rank or position
4. humble	D. understand and enjoy
5. impression	E. important

II. Decide whether the following statements are true or false according to Passage II.

1. When a European boss says "Good job." to you, he really means it. (　　)

2. The Pakistani does not think "Good job." is a strong praise. (　　)

3. Europeans dislike Americans in that the latter give too much positive feedback. (　　)

4. Don't take it very seriously when a Pakistan says "Thank you." to you. (　　)

5. Americans appreciate your work because they think you don't have to work for them. (　　)

III. Fill in the blanks in following passage with words from Passage II.

Americans believe that everyone is 1_____ though they don't believe all the people are the same. They are under no obligation while working. The boss only 2_____ your work when he says "Good job." to you. It is just good 3_____ to express appreciation. So if you come from a different culture, you can be easily 4_____ and get the wrong idea about your job performance. Therefore, it is very 5_____ to learn cultural differences.

 **Passage III**

88.2% of People Travel the World to Get Their Hands on This...

Think Before Reading

1. What do you think of the role of food in tourism?

2. Do you think food is an art?

3. Have you ever been to any food festivals?

Can a meal alter your perspective or offer you profound insight?

You have probably heard the saying, *we eat with our eyes*. Presentation (展示) affects how attractive a dish appears — a beautifully presented dish can wet our hunger, while a sloppily (马马虎虎地) plated dish can sour it. These days, with foodie (美食家) culture featuring (使有特色) so popularly in the media, the standards for what is expected of restaurants is higher than ever. People are travelling far to find new and exciting flavors.

The increase of food photography (摄影) and recipe sharing on social media has stimulated a wide appreciation of food visually. Food cinematography (摄影) attracts viewers with up-close shots and creeping (爬行的) camera rolls over table spreads.

When people actually sit down to enjoy a delicious meal, many of them preserve the experience through photographs. These photographs are indicators of the diner's tastes, class, sense of refinement (精致) and adventurous attitude. When people go on vacation, you will be able to spot the food-conscious traveler by the ratio of exotic (异国情调的) food photographs there are in their albums compared to photographs of sites and people. People treat their consumption of foreign food in much the same way that they would treat their visit of a famous architectural structure or painting.

With this shift towards a visual and symbolic appreciation of food, critics are taking the role of food in the art world into consideration. And if chefs are masters of the art of cooking and food is their artistic medium, can food in and of itself be considered art?

Many people readily call cooking an art form but where actual food itself is concerned, there is still debate.

In his lecture, "Is Food Art?", Dr. Ken Albala of the University of the Pacific makes the observation that a distinct label has been given to food that is artfully crafted: artisanal (手工艺性的).

The demand for craft food and drinks has certainly risen, with diners and home cooks seeking food that is less processed, with a more authentic, farm-to-table feel. Giant restaurant chains have responded to this trend by re-branding their menus to offer "artisanal" products, such as Starbucks' purchase of La Boulange's (法国著名烘焙品牌) recipes, which helped drive a 16% increase in their food sales. People are willing to pay higher prices for foods that reflect craftsmanship and quality.

The Rise of Food Tourism

People willingly travel across oceans to see the Mona Lisa in the flesh. They will pay thousands of dollars to walk under the ceiling of the Sistine Chapel (意大利西斯廷礼拜堂). The history, mythology and reputation that surround famous art pieces have the power to inspire people

to want to see them in person. Twentieth century philosopher and cultural critic Walter Benjamin called this transcendent (超验的) power of the original art piece its "aura" (特质).

It has become common now for people to take entire trips dedicated to trying local cuisines of different countries. Food tourism has increased greatly in popularity in recent years. People seek out foreign foods in the same way that they seek out other elements of foreign cultures like art, music and architecture.

The dishes served at world-renowned restaurants possess much the same "aura" as famous art or architecture. But this "aura" can also surround certain typical local dishes, like paella (海鲜炒饭) in Spain. What this means is that such dishes do not have to be found on expensive tasting menus — they can also be found in the markets and homes of locals.

According to a 2012 World Tourism Organization report, 88.2% of survey respondents (调查对象) consider food a defining element of the brand image of travel destinations.

The report also revealed that over a third of tourist spending is devoted to food. This is a trend in tourism that has risen over the past decade. A study by *The American Culinary* (烹饪的) *Traveler* showed that the percentage of US leisure travelers who seek to learn about unique dining experiences on their travels rose from 40% to 51% between 2006 and 2013.

One of the primary reasons travelers are so interested in sampling the food and food culture of different countries is, aside from the discovery of new flavors, so that they can participate in the local community. They are travelers seeking the authenticity of the places they visit through food. They are concerned about the origin of products. They recognize the value of gastronomy (烹调法) as a means of socializing, as a space for sharing life with others.

Throughout history, people have travelled to attend music festivals, to take part in the shared enjoyment of music. Now people also travel for food festivals. The Melbourne Food and Wine Festival pulls in an attendance of over 250,000 each year. The Maine Lobster Festival draws in a crowd of 30,000, while the San Francisco Street Food Festival draws a crowd of around 50,000 yearly.

In the UNWTO report, Catherine Gazzoli, Chief Executive Officer of Slow Food UK says, "Culinary tourism does not have to mean delicious food. It is increasingly about unique and memorable experiences. It helps to diversify revenue (收入) sources, and improves rural employment and income levels."

For many travelers, food tourism is about what food represents for a culture-local aesthetics (唯美) of flavor, conventions of presentation, and the ideologies (思想观念) behind ingredients, preparation, and eating practices. This puts the spotlight not just on master chefs, but also on local artisans. Similar to how the attitude towards street art has shifted in the mainstream art community, so has the mainstream attitude towards street food, market food and home cooking.

Think of how many travel albums feature photos taken in markets and small cafes-lively fruit stands, tables of smooth and shiny fish, shelves of golden pastries (点心). By stopping to appreciate these foods and snap a photo of them, tourists consider these foods as art objects. Becoming addicted to a certain kind of food is like becoming addicted to a certain style of music — it leaves a lasting impression on the person who consumes it and inspires them to seek a deeper intellectual and sensory (感官的) understanding of it.

Towards More Utilitarian (实用的) Art

The acceptance of food as art broadens the realm of possibility for other crafts and creations that serve a utilitarian purpose to be considered art too.

Dr. Ken Albala comes to a beautiful conclusion in his lecture, and it's a good way to tie up this article as well:

"It should be considered a highest form of art not because it's fancy and elegant or rare and exotic but because we have to eat it regularly, and we experience food not just in the moment that it hits our palate (味觉), but of course it courses through our bodies. It's the only art that actually becomes us, physically, emotionally, spiritually, and what other kind of art could aspire to such an essential place for our species?"

Food, like art, can be tasted and digested two ways: you can try to explain it, or you can let the experience wash over you. Both ways will leave a lasting impression on you and within you.

I. Choose the best choice to answer or finish each of the following questions.

1. What is the author's attitude toward the food tourism?

    A. Positive.   B. Negative.   C. Neutral.   D. Suspicious.

2. What is the influence of the popularity of food tourism on the critics?

    A. They disagree that food is an art.

    B. They regard cooking as well as food a kind of art.

    C. They are holding a debate on food tourism.

    D. They begin to think about whether food is an art.

3. Why did Starbucks buy the recipe of La Boulage?

    A. Because French snacks are more popular in coffee shops.

    B. Because the customers are pursing artisanal foods.

    C. Because people value band more than quality.

    D. Because La Boulage recipes are expensive.

4. What is the new tendency in tourism over the past decade?

    A. Food industry develops fast internationally.

    B. Food is the only reason for tourists traveling.

    C. Food costs are increasing among tourists.

    D. Food culture is more attractive than sightseeing.

5. Why are tourists keen on food?

    A. Because they want to be master chefs themselves.

    B. Because they are keen on the exotic flavor of other countries.

    C. Because they want to introduce exotic food to their own countries.

    D. Because they would like to get in touch with the local culture.

II. Match the words with their definitions.

WORDS	DEFINITIONS
1. indicator	A. unable to stop taking
2. exotic	B. use of goods and services to satisfy needs
3. chef	C. a skilled cook, especially the main cook in a hotel or restaurant
4. consumption	D. something seems unusual and interesting because it is related to a foreign country
5. addicted	E. something that can be regarded as a sign of something else

III. Decide whether the following statements are true or false according to Passage III.

1. The appearance of more pictures shared in social media reflects the popularity of food tourism. (   )

2. According to Dr. Ken Albala, cooking is an art form but food is not. (   )

3. The food tourists care for the "aura" of food rather than the food itself. (   )

4. The foods that tourists seek can be found in the famous restaurants as well as local markets. (   )

5. More tourists value the craftsmanship more than the quality in food. (   )

6. Many people travel abroad to attend food festivals just like attending music festivals. (   )

7. According to Catherine Gazzoli, food tourists help to improve local economy. (   )

8. Street food, market food and home cooking cannot represent the mainstream characteristics of local food. (   )

9. According to the author, food consumption is both aesthetic and utilitarian. (   )

10. The author agrees that food is the highest form of art. (   )

Unit 3

Sightseeing

Life is like a journey, don't care about the destination, but the scenery and the mood at the view. Sightseeing is a good way to refresh and broaden your horizon (视野). During the journey, you can turn off your cellphone and keep far from the Internet. You can forget your work or your study, and just enjoy the leisure time. From the moment when you start your journey, all the trifles (琐事) should be locked at your house. During the travel, you can see different scenic spots and contact with different people. They may be a window for you to know a different world.

Passage I

Dali

Think Before Reading

1. Which city will you choose to be your next travel destination?
2. Do you know the city of Dali?
3. What would you like to do if you travel in Dali?

Dali City is a county-level city in Dali, Yunnan Province, China. It is one of Yunnan's most popular tourist destinations, both for its historic sites and the "Foreigners' Street" that features western-style food, music, and English-speaking business owners, making it popular among both western and Chinese tourists. Dali is located on a fertile (肥沃的) plateau (高原) between Mount Cangshan to the west and Erhai Lake to the east. It has traditionally been settled by the Bai and Yi minorities (少数民族). It is also the capital of the Dali Bai Autonomous Prefecture (大理白族自治州). Dali is also famous for producing the many types of marble (大理石),

which are used primarily in construction and for decorative objects. In fact, Dali is so famous for the stone that the name of marble in Chinese is literally (字面地) "Dali Stone".

Three Pagodas (塔), about one kilometer northwest of the ancient city of Dali, occupying a scenic location at the foot of Mount Cangshan facing Erhai Lake, has a history of over 1,800 years. It is a symbol of the history of Dali City, and a record of the development of Buddhism (佛教) in

the area. As its name implies, Three Pagodas are made of three ancient independent pagodas forming a symmetrical (对称的) triangle. This is unique in China. A visit to the Three Pagodas should not be missed by any visitor to Dali City. Today, travelers can visit the Three Pagodas at night, when it is illuminated (照亮) providing a fantastic scene. Nearby on the "marble street" there are many folk-craft workshops and stands specializing in marble and brick-painting.

Erhai Lake is the largest highland lake and one of the seven biggest fresh water lakes in China. The lake covers an area of 250 square kilometers and is located about two kilometers east of Dali.

The beautiful scenery and limpid (清澈的) waters of Erhai Lake are charming and attractive. The picturesque scenery makes you feel relaxed and happy. During a clear night, the moon is mirrored in the lake and people call it the "Erhai Moon" which is one of the four best sights of Dali. It would be a great pity if people travelling to Dali do not go for a boat ride in the lake, just like people travelling to Kunming without having a glance at the scenery of the Western Hills.

Mount Cangshan is a high mountain rising above the city of Dali in the southern area of Yunnan that borders Vietnam (越南). It is a scenic spot and a good hiking area where hikers may bring tents. There are 18 peaks on this mountain that are all over 3,500 meters in altitude, and the highest summit named Malong is 4,122 meters high. The mountain is noted for its very rich and diverse flora (植物群).There are cable cars up the mountain, and a road connects various sites of interests. The mountain is a highlight of the Dali area,

with numerous springs, ponds and waterfalls, beautiful scenery, hiking trails, a range of ecological zones with thousands of plant species, and scenic views of lakes and the city of Dali.

Not only Chinese people, but also foreign tourists are attracted by Dali in Yunnan Province. They are so absorbed in the ancient customs and the historic culture that they even aspire (渴望) to live in Dali for a long time. Gradually, there is a road which is full of western tourists inside of Dali City named "Yangren Street (Foreigner Street)". If you like shopping, this street is your best choice. This place gathers a variety of crafts and textiles made by the local Bai people. Many antique shops will give you some extra surprises.

I. Choose the best choice to answer or finish each of the following questions.

1. This article is probably chosen from a/an _____.

   A. entertainment magazine   B. travel journal

   C. geography textbook   D. newspaper

2. Which of the following statements about Dali city is NOT true?

   A. It is the capital of the Dali Bai Autonomous Prefecture.

   B. It is a popular tourist destination for the historic sites.

   C. It is famous for selling a variety of marbles in ancient times.

   D. It is located on a plateau between a mountain and a lake.

3. Which of the following places is NOT a tourist spot of Dali?

    A. Erhai Lake.   B. Three Pagodas.

    C. Mount Cangshan.   D. Western Hills.

4. Why do Three Pagodas become a must-visit place in Dali?

    A. Its symmetrical triangle form is unique in China.

    B. It has charming and fantastic scenery.

    C. It is a highlight of the Dali area.

    D. It has many antique shops which will give travelers surprises.

5. Which of the following things does NOT belong to Mount Cangshan?

    A. Diverse flora.   B. Cable car.

    C. Numerous springs.   D. Limpid waters.

II. Match the words with their definitions.

WORDS	DEFINITIONS
1. destination	A. having beautiful natural scenery
2. scenic	B. being the only one of its kind
3. feature	C. to make sb./sth. come somewhere or take part in sth.
4. unique	D. a place to which sb./sth. is going or being sent
5. attract	E. something important or typical of a place or thing

III. Please list at least three places travelers should visit in Dali, and give the reasons.

1. _____.

2. _____.

3. _____.

The Eiffel Tower

Think Before Reading

1. How popular is the Eiffel Tower in the world?
2. What's the basic information of the Eiffel Tower?

The Eiffel Tower is a wrought (锻造的) iron lattice (格子框架) tower on the Champ de Mars in Paris, France. It is named after the engineer Gustave Eiffel, whose company designed and built the tower.

Constructed from 1887 to 1889 as the entrance to the 1889 World's Fair, it was initially (最初) criticized by some of France's leading artists and intellectuals (知识分子) for its design, but it has become a global cultural icon (偶像) of France and one of the most recognizable structures in the world. The Eiffel Tower is the most-visited paid monument (纪念碑) in the world; 6.91 million people ascended (攀登) it in 2015.

The tower is 324 metres tall, about the same height as an 81-storey building, and the tallest structure in Paris. Its base is square, measuring 125 metres on each side. During its construction, the Eiffel Tower surpassed the Washington Monument to become the tallest man-made structure in the world, a title it held for 41 years until the Chrysler Building in New York City was finished in 1930. Due to the addition of a broadcasting aerial (天线) at the top of the tower in 1957, it is now taller than the Chrysler Building by 5.2 metres. Excluding transmitters (除了发射器), the Eiffel Tower is the second tallest structure in France after the Millau Viaduct.

The tower has three levels for visitors, with restaurants on the first and second levels. The top level's upper platform is 276 metres above the ground — the highest observation deck accessible to the public in the European Union. Tickets can be purchased to ascend by stairs or lift to the first and second levels. The climb from ground level to the first level is over 300 steps, as is the climb from the first level to the second. Although there is a staircase to the top level, it is usually accessible only by lift.

More than 250 million people have visited the tower since it was completed in 1889. The tower is the most-visited paid monument in the world. An average of 25,000 people ascend the tower every day which can result in long queues.

The tower has two restaurants: Le 58 Tour Eiffel on the first level, and Le Jules Verne, a gourmet (美食家) restaurant with its own lift on the second level. This restaurant has one star in *the Michelin Red Guide*. It is run by the multi-Michelin star chef Alain Ducasse and owes its name to the famous science-fiction writer Jules Verne. Additionally, there is a champagne bar at the top of the Eiffel Tower.

As one of the most iconic landmarks in the world, the Eiffel Tower has been the inspiration

for the creation of many replicas (复制品) and similar towers. An early example is Blackpool Tower in England. The mayor of Blackpool, Sir John Bickerstaffe, was so impressed on seeing the Eiffel Tower at the 1889 exposition that he commissioned (委任) a similar tower to be built in his town. It opened in 1894 and is 158.1 metres tall. Tokyo Tower in Japan, built as a communications tower in 1958, was also inspired by the Eiffel Tower.

There are various scale models of the tower in the United States, including a half-scale version at the Paris Las Vegas, Nevada, one in Paris, Texas built in 1993, and two 1:3 scale models at Kings Island, Ohio, and Kings Dominion, Virginia, amusement parks opened in 1972 and 1975 respectively.

In 2011, the TV show *Pricing the Priceless* on the National Geographic Channel speculated (估价) that a full-size replica of the tower would cost approximately US$480 million to build.

I. Match the words with their definitions.

WORDS	DEFINITIONS
1. accessible	A. to build or make sth. such as a road, building or machine
2. criticize	B. something being important as a symbol
3. icon	C. to do or be better than sb./sth.
4. construct	D. find fault with
5. surpass	E. capable of being reached

II. Decide whether the following statements are true or false according to Passage II.

1. The Eiffel Tower being built as the entrance to the 1889 World's Fair impressed everyone initially. (   )
2. The Eiffel Tower surpassed the Washington Monument to become the tallest man-made structure in the world until even nowadays. (   )
3. The climb from ground level to the second level is over 600 steps. (   )
4. The restaurant Le Jules Verne with its own lift locates on the second level of the Eiffel Tower. (   )
5. As speculated by the TV show *Pricing the Priceless,* the Eiffel Tower is worth about US$480 million. (   )

III. Fill in the blanks in following passage with words from Passage II.

Built as the entrance to the 1889 World's Fair, the Eiffel Tower was initially 1_____ by some of artists and intellectuals. However it has become a global cultural 2_____ of France and been visited by millions of people all over the world every year. The Eiffel Tower was once the tallest building in the world, but is the second tallest 3_____ in France now. Tower restaurants are located on the first and second 4_____ of the tower. There are many replicas of the tower in the world, but it will be very 5_____ to build a full-size one.

Passage III

Discovering Suzhou: Background and Classical Gardens

Think Before Reading

1. Have you ever traveled to Suzhou?

2. Do you know the history of Suzhou?

3. Can you name some classical gardens in Suzhou?

(A) Built in 514 BC, Suzhou is an ancient city with 2,500 years' history, located in the center of Yangtze Delta (长江三角洲) near Shanghai. It covers a land area of 8,488.42 km² and 1,649.72 km² is the urban area, more than six million people now live in Suzhou.

(B) The unique characteristics of the past are still retained (保留) in present-day Suzhou. It is renowned for the classic gardens, canals, silks, lakes, operas, legends and museums… and yet, there is so much more. From natural and man-made heritage to modern creations; from cultural gems (瑰宝) to natural oases (绿洲); from great arts to daily lives, nothing is missed. It's strongly recommended to dig a little deeper, and experience classic Suzhou.

The History and Legends of the City

(C) Suzhou is a land of classic legends, ranging from the world's oldest cross-continental trade routes to the most influential military book in ancient China. Marco Polo, probably the most famous

Western traveler, traveled on the Silk Road and visited Suzhou in 1276. According to his words, Suzhou was then dotted with bridges, rich in silk production and renowned for its elaborate handicrafts. The Art of War, a Chinese military treatise (论著) written by Sun Tzu (孙子) in Suzhou (at that time known as the State of Wu) during the Spring and Autumn period (600 BC), was later widely implemented (实施) in both Asian and Western culture and politics.

(D) The classic legends of Suzhou began as early as the 21st century BC when King Wu (also known as Taibo) made Suzhou the capital of the State of Wu. It is said in history that realizing that his younger brother, Jili, was wiser than him, and deserved to inherit the throne, Taibo, the eldest son of King Zhou, fled to Suzhou and established the State of Wu.

(E) As time passed by, the classic legends of Suzhou developed in different fields. Exquisite (精美的) carving works on miniature objects such as grains of rice or individual beans, Suzhou silk embroideries (刺绣), Chinese paintings on fans and Kun Opera (昆曲) are just a few examples. Wang Shuyuan, a Suzhou local craftsman in the Ming Dynasty, managed to carve on a 3.3-centimeter long walnut with a vivid picture of a boat including windows, a tea pot, a stove, five people and 24 Chinese characters inside. Also in the Ming Dynasty, a talented Chinese painter called Tang Bohu spent most of his life in Suzhou. In time, Suzhou Classical Gardens, lakes and mountains, and the lifestyles of local scholars became common subjects in his paintings.

Classical Gardens of Suzhou

(F) The ancient city of Suzhou has an enviable location and trading history that has resulted in a unique level of prosperity (繁荣) and fortune through the ages. Perhaps the greatest result of this can be seen in the breathtaking and historical Suzhou classical gardens. It is little wonder that people say South China is the most beautiful, and Suzhou is the most beautiful in South China. People from Suzhou are

undoubtedly proud of their unique heritage. These world famous classical gardens are important not just in China, but worldwide. The Suzhou classical gardens are UNESCO World Heritage listed and are the reason why the city has become one of the most revered (受崇敬的) cities in China.

The Humble Administrator's Garden (拙政园)

(G) The Humble Administrator's Garden is considered the greatest of all southern Chinese gardens. During the reign of Emperor Zhengde, the site was occupied by Dahong Temple. At that time, a censor (御史) named Wang Xianchen appropriated (占用) the temple and converted it into a private villa, but the Wang family could not maintain the garden and sold it a few years later. In the coming centuries the garden repeatedly changed hands and was reconstructed many times, so the garden we see today is far removed from the one enjoyed by Wang Xianchen.

(H) The entire site was once a piece of level swampy (沼泽) land. When the garden was first constructed, the earth was scooped to make lakes and piled up to make islands. Despite its beauty, the garden fared badly in the later Ming Dynasty. The eastern portion was parceled off while western and central halves became the villas of government officials. Neglect continued until the reigns of Emperor Shunzhi and Kangxi of the Qing Dynasty, when the garden was extensively repaired. The changes in the Kangxi period were particularly great, modifying whole portions of the plan.

(I) During Emperor Qianlong's reign, the garden was again divided into two parts; the western being the Shu Yuan (Book of Study Garden) and the eastern being the "Restored Garden" (Fu Yuan). Repairs to the garden continued throughout the Qing Dynasty, but the appearance of today closely resembles how the garden appeared in the late Qing. However, the eastern portion of the garden only joined the center in 1949 when modifications (修缮) were made to the eastern side.

The Lingering Garden (留园)

(J) The Lingering Garden is located outside the Changmen Gate (阊门) of Suzhou. Buildings, the primary feature of any Chinese garden, occupy one third of the total area. A unique feature of this garden is the 700 m covered walk which connects them. The built elements of the garden are grouped by sections. "Central section", the ensemble (总体) of structures in the central garden encircles a pond and grotto (岩洞) main feature. The grotto is constructed of yellow granite (花岗

岩) and was created by the noted artist Zhou Binzhong. The eastern section of the garden is arrayed (排列) around the cloud capped peak stone (云顶石). A central courtyard is ringed by buildings.

(K) Behind the Old Hermit Scholars' House is the Small Court of Stone Forest, a collection of scholar stones and connected minor courtyards. The western section is mostly natural, containing only a few pavilions, a large artificial hill, and a Bonsai garden.

The Master-of-Nets Garden (网师园)

(L) The Master-of-Nets Garden is one of the four famous gardens in Suzhou, which has also won the titles of world cultural heritage site. The garden demonstrates Chinese garden designers' adept (精湛的) skills for synthesizing (综合的) art, nature, and architecture to create unique metaphysical (超自然的) masterpieces. The initial garden was first constructed over 800 years ago and even though its physical form has changed drastically (彻底地) since, the name and spirit of the garden still remain intact (完好的). The Master-of-Nets Garden is particularly regarded among garden connoisseurs (鉴赏家) for its mastering the techniques of relative dimension (尺寸), contrast, foil (衬托), sequence (排列) and depth, and borrowed scenery. While the garden's primary uses have varied over time, its ability to inspire visitors intellectually and spiritually remains unchanged. Keen physical architecture combined with poetic and artistic inspirations makes the Master-of-Nets garden a unique and incredible garden experience that has stood the test of time.

The Lion-Grove Garden (狮子林)

(M) The Lion-Grove Garden, built in the Yuan Dynasty, is famous for its rockeries (假山), most of which look like lions, hence the name. It is small but well arranged and to the southeast there are hills while in the northwest there is water.

(N) Around the garden there is a walkway that follows the contours (轮廓) of the land and there are a number of buildings that are in perfect harmony with the scenery including Yanyu Hall, Sleeping- Clouds Chamber and Seed-Plum-Blossoms Tower.

I. Choose the best choice to answer or finish each of the following questions.

1. Suzhou is renowned for the following items EXCEPT _____.

   A. canals   B. gardens   C. bridges   D. silks

2. What has resulted in the prosperity and fortune of Suzhou in the ancient China?

   A. Its location.   B. Its legend.   C. Its history.   D. Its visitors.

3. Which of the following gardens is considered the greatest of all southern Chinese gardens?

   A. The Humble Administrator's Garden.   B. The Lingering Garden.

   C. The Master-of-Nets Garden.   D. The Lion-Grove Garden.

4. A unique feature of the Lingering Garden is _____.

   A. the built elements being grouped by sections

   B. the covered walk which connects the buildings

   C. the central garden which encircles a pond and grotto

   D. the eastern section being arrayed around the cloud capped peak stone

5. How did the Lion-Grove Garden get its name?

   A. It is small but well arranged.

   B. A number of buildings are in perfect harmony with the scenery.

   C. There are hills to the southeast while there is water in the northwest.

   D. Most of its rockeries look like lions.

II. Match the words with their definitions.

WORDS	DEFINITION
1. retain	A. producing very clear pictures in your mind
2. vivid	B. the way that sb./sth. looks on the outside
3. fortune	C. to show sth. clearly by giving proof or evidence
4. appearance	D. chance or luck, especially in the way it affects people's lives
5. demonstrate	E. to keep sth.; to continue to have sth.

III. Identify the paragraph from which the information is derived.

_____ 1. Suzhou is a respectable city since its classical gardens are on the World Heritage listed.

_____ 2. A unique feature of the Lingering Garden is the covered walk which connects the buildings.

_____ 3. It is worthwhile to visit Suzhou deeply for its classic characteristics.

_____ 4. The Humble Administrator's Garden today is different from that in the Ming Dynasty.

_____ 5. Suzhou was the capital of the State of Wu in the 21st century BC.

_____ 6. Sun Tzu's *The Art of War* also had influence on Western culture and politics.

_____ 7. The Humble Administrator's Garden once was neglected in history.

_____ 8. The Lion-Grove Garden is named after the shape of its rockeries.

_____ 9. The Master-of-Nets Garden demonstrates the designer's exquisite skills.

_____ 10. The common subjects of Tang Bohu's paintings were the classical scenery of Suzhou.

Unit 4

Accommodation

Lead-in

An accommodation is a place that can accommodate human beings. It can mean a room or place where you will stay or an agreement about sharing something. Many accommodations are for overnight stays, but this is not a mandatory (强制性的) requirement. For there are more specific types of accommodations one can use. Tourist Accommodation means the business of marketing or providing accommodation to paying guests, and includes hotel businesses, hostels, beds and breakfasts, recreational vehicle parks, and tree-houses.

Capsule (胶囊) Hotel

Think Before Reading

1. Do you have any experiences of living in hotels?
2. What are your requirements for a hotel?
3. What is your feeling of sleeping in an enclosed space?

A capsule hotel, also known as a pod hotel, is a type of hotel developed in Japan that features (使有……特色) a large number of extremely small "rooms" (capsules) intended to provide cheap,

basic overnight accommodation for guests who do not require or who cannot afford the services offered by more conventional (传统的) hotels.

The concept of a capsule hotel first took root in Japan in 1979, but now they are also found in China and Singapore. These are very low-budget (低成本的，低预算的) lodgings (住处) that feature modular (模块化的) plastic or fiberglass (玻璃纤维) blocks stacked (垛起来)

one over the other. These blocks are in the form of small capsules, which can house only one person at a time. Meant primarily for an overnight stay, these provide very basic facilities, like a sleeping mattress and television set.

The guest room is a modular plastic or fiberglass block roughly 2 by 1 by 1.25 m (6 ft 7 in by 3 ft 3 in by 4 ft 1 in). Facilities differ, but most include a television, an electronic console (控制板), and wireless Internet connection. The capsules are stacked side-by-side, two units high, with steps providing access to the second level rooms. The open end of the capsule can be closed for privacy, with a curtain or a fibreglass door. Luggage is stored in a locker; and washrooms are communal (公用的). Guests are asked not to smoke or eat in the capsules. Some hotels also provide restaurants [or at least vending machines (自动售货机)], pools, and other entertainment facilities. Capsule hotels vary in size, from 50 or so capsules to 700, and they are used primarily by men. Some capsule hotels offer separate sections for male and female guests. Clothes and shoes can sometimes be exchanged for a yukata (浴衣) and

slippers on entry. A towel may also be provided.

The benefit of these hotels is convenience and low price, usually around JP¥2,000–4,000 (USD 18–36) a night. They provide an alternative for those who (especially on weeknights) may be too drunk to return home safely, or too embarrassed to face their spouses. With continued recession (不景气) in Japan, as of early 2010, more and more guests were unemployed who had become homeless during the crisis and were temporarily

renting capsules by the month. This style of hotel has not gained wide popularity outside Japan, although Western variants (变体) known as "pod hotels" have been developed, with larger accommodations and often private baths.

The particular capsule hotel is located near Kabukicho in the Shinjuku area of Tokyo. It allows only men. It cost JP¥3,800 for the "room" and bath. Massages (按摩) are available for an additional JP¥3,300 for 40 minutes. It's on the 6th floor of a building and is called Big Lemon. It's open 24 hours and you can leave and come back as you wish.

They speak a little English and foreigners are welcome. You can store your luggage behind the counter. You pay at a vending machine and hand the ticket to the clerk. They give you a capsule number and locker key and wrist band. When you are in for the night, you change in the locker room and wear the small yukata around the facility. Upstairs is a shower and sento bath (森脱浴，一种公共浴). There is a restaurant and small bar as well. Beside that is a TV room with several lazy boy chairs. Technically you could pay only JP¥1,200 for the sento and sleep in the lazy boy chairs as many people were doing.

Since most visitors to a capsule hotel are Japanese business men who don't have time to go

home, there are amenities (便利设施) there for people who didn't plan on staying away from home. You can shave, brush your teeth, take a bath, buy shirts, pants, belts, ties, undershirts. Not sure if there is overnight dry-cleaning, but I wouldn't doubt it. Check-out was around 9 am and starting at 7 am. They made public announcements reminding people to get up and get out. There were about 150 capsules in this facility. Some

have 600+ in Shinjuku.

There are many buttons and knobs in the capsule. One turns on the light and a knob dims the light. One turns on the TV, another button flips through the channels. There is a radio and an alarm clock built in. At the end of the capsule there is a screen you can pull down to "lock" yourself in. The entire capsule was about 6 to 6.5 feet long. The building was slightly warmer than I prefer. I wish there were individual heaters/coolers in each capsule.

I. Choose the best choice to answer or finish each of the following questions.

1. The function of a capsule hotel is to _____.

   A. offer a luxurious accommodation in a small hotel

   B. get the patients cured by the doctors and recover sooner

   C. provide an inexpensive overnight stay in a narrow place

   D. keep the dead body in a safe and enclosed place

2. The facilities in the capsules do not include _____.

   A. radio   B. television   C. mattress   D. couch

3. Capsule hotels are popular in Japan because of _____.

   A. the economic recession

   B. the rising divorce rate

   C. the easy check-in

   D. the low managing cost

4. Who are the main customers to the capsule hotel in Japan?

   A. The workers who do not plan to go home.

   B. The business men who can't return home.

   C. The drunken clerks who are not married.

   D. The peasants who have just arrived in the city.

5. The word "lock" in the last paragraph means "_____".

   A. to turn off the TV set inside

   B. to lock up the capsule from inside

   C. to be enclosed in the capsule

   D. to turn off the light inside

II. Match the words with their definitions.

WORDS	DEFINITIONS
1. stack	A. not bright, not clearly to be seen
2. remind	B. to move quickly
3. dim	C. to pile up
4. flip	D. to make someone remember
5.prefer	E. to like something or someone more

III. Decide whether the following statements are true or false according to Passage I.

1. Capsule hotels are originated from Japan. (   )

2. Hotel guests may put their belongings in the capsule. (   )

3. Only men are allowed in the capsule hotels near Kabukicho in the Shinjuku area. (   )

4. Capsule hotels are popular all around the world. (   )

5. Capsule hotel rooms are big enough to hold tall people. (   )

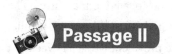 **Passage II**

Vacation Rentals

旅游英语 泛读

Think Before Reading

1. Who is the owner of the "vocational rentals"?
2. What's the difference between the "vocational rentals" and the timeshare?
3. Why are vacation rentals banned in many places?

A vacation rental is the renting out of a furnished (布置好的) apartment, house, or professionally managed resort-condominium complex (联排别墅) on a temporary basis to tourists as an alternative to a hotel.

Vacation rentals have long been a popular travel option in Europe as well as in Canada and are becoming increasingly popular across the world.

Vacation rentals usually occur in privately owned vacation properties (房地产) (holiday homes), so the variety of accommodation is broad and inconsistent (不一致的). The property is a fully furnished property, such as a holiday villa, apartment, cottage, condominium, townhome or single-family-style home. Farm stay can encompass (包含) participation (参与) on a working farm, or a more conventional rental that happens to be co-located on a farm. The client/traveler arranges to rent the vacation rental property for a designated (指定的) period of time. Some rent on a nightly basis similar to hotel rooms, although the more prevalent (流行的) vacation rental industry practice is typically weekly rentals.

Vacation rentals can range from budget studio apartments to lavish (奢华的), expensive private villas (别墅) in the world's most desirable locations, some with price tags of many thousands per night and all the facilities you would find in any luxury accommodation to cater (供应饮食) to the guests.

Some vacation rentals, particularly condominiums or apartments, offer many of the same services hotels offer to their guests, e.g., front desk check-in, 24-hour maintenance, in-house housekeeping, and concierge (看门人) service.

Villa holidays are very popular in Europe, and main destinations include the United States Virgin Islands, Italy, Spain, France, Germany, Greece, and Turkey.

Vacation rentals are available in most states of the US and is prevalent in major tourist areas such as Florida, Hawaii and California, as well as in other coastal areas with beaches, where they may be referred to as beach houses, many of which are rentals. The vacation rental market is much larger in Europe than in the United States, and Florida is a popular destination for villa holidays for Europeans.

Consumers unfamiliar with the concept of a vacation rental may confuse it with the seemingly similar, but distinctly different, timeshare. Many timeshare resorts offer quarter ownership, which provides 13 weeks of use or rental.

A timeshare can still be made available as a vacation rental should an owner decide to put his owned week(s) on a vacation rental program. Also, a large segment of the 21% of unsold and therefore still resort-controlled inventory (存货总值) is made available as vacation rentals. In 2014, this was a $1.9 billion business.

A timeshare is a piece of real estate (不动产) — often a fully furnished condominium — that is jointly shared by several owners. While different types of timeshare ownerships exist, in general, each owner bears a part of the responsibility, along with the right to a part of time in which he or she is granted sole use of the property. Timeshare resorts allow financially qualified guests to rent

and tour (到……旅游) their unowned properties and then make those properties available to the guest for purchase. Timeshare owners can also choose to bank (积累) their week with an exchange company or rent the unit.

Traditional hotels generally do not include vacation properties. However, some contemporary resort developments (度假设施发展项目) include shared ownership components (成分) such as villas and condominiums that can be either rented through the hotel or rented out by their owners either directly or through agencies.

Some travelers avoid vacation rentals for fear of what industry insiders call SNAD: "Significantly Not As Described". This refers to a property that looks like paradise(天堂) in the photos, only to reveal leaky (漏雨的) roofs and blocked views upon the traveler's arrival. To reduce this risk, many vacation rental companies offer user reviews.

Another significant concern is that people may create false accounts, and advertise vacation homes which they do not in fact own. This can lead to unsuspecting (不怀疑的) customers booking and paying for a vacation, only to find on arrival that the rental does not exist. Given that the accommodation has been booked and paid for many months in advance, the culprit (罪犯) may disappear without trace, leaving the customer out of pocket.

In many counties, towns and cities, local authorities attempt to regulate (规范) or ban (禁止) vacation rentals after complaints from local residents or competing lodging businesses. In the United States, New York City, Chicago and other cities have introduced restrictions on short term rentals, though regulation is not always strictly enforced. The City of Portland, for example, does not allow rentals of less than 30 days in residential zones; however, according to local vacation property managers such as Vacasa, the average guest stays 3 – 10 nights.

In most US cities and counties, zoning ordinances (分区规划条例) prohibit (禁止) any type of lodging business in areas zoned for residential use. In some areas, zoning allows limited lodging uses provided (假如) that they are secondary to the primary residential use of the property.

I. Match the words with their definitions.

WORDS	DEFINITIONS
1. occur	A. relating to homes rather than offices or businesses
2. furnish	B. to make someone cannot think clearly or do not understand
3. range	C. variety of things/people
4. confuse	D. to put furniture in a house/room
5. residential	E. to happen

II. Choose the best choice to answer or finish each of the following questions.

1. The passage mainly introduces _____.

   A. vacation rentals

   B. traditional hotels

   C. time shares

   D. different hotels

2. Most vacation rentals are rented by the _____.

   A. day   B. month   C. year   D. hour

3. What's the difference between vacation rentals and timeshares?

   A. Timeshares offer part of ownership.

   B. Timeshares offer the complete ownership.

   C. Timeshares do not include vacation properties.

   D. Timeshare owners cannot lease the houses.

4. How can people reduce the risk of being cheated by vacation rental companies according to the passage?

   A. Never pay for it before arrival.

   B. Believe the SNAD vacation rentals.

   C. Refer to more user reviews.

   D. Visit the spot before moving in.

5. Some vacation rentals are restricted in some cities of America because _____.

   A. they do not have hotel business licenses

   B. the local hotels are more popular by the tourists

   C. some local residents often complain about them

   D. the local regulations are not strictly enforced

III. Fill in the blanks in following passage with words from Passage II.

      A vacation rental is a vacation choice for 1_____. The sizes and locations may be 2_____. They are more 3_____ in Europe than in America. Vacation rentals are different from the timeshares according to their ownership although timeshares could still 4_____ their shares. In most US cities and counties, the local governments do not allow any type of lodging business in 5_____ areas. In some areas, vacation rentals are permitted only if they are secondary to the primary residential use of the property.

What Do Hotel Stars Really Mean?

Think Before Reading

1. Do you have any experiences of living in 5-star hotels?
2. Are you clear about the specific standard of starred hotels?
3. Are there any 7-star hotels in the world?

While the problem of hotel-star inflation (夸张) isn't exactly a pressing world issue, it does feel a lot like a game of grade-school one-upmanship (胜人一筹的本领) that will inevitably end with the world's first "Infinity-Plus-One-Star" (无限加一星) hotel, probably somewhere in Dubai. But with all the talk of super-starred hotels, one is left to wonder: who exactly is assigning (分派) all these stars? And what do they mean? AND WHEN WILL THE MADNESS END? We wanted to know the answers to at least two of those questions and now we'd like to share that new knowledge with you. Here's everything you need to know about the hotel star system.

Who Makes the Ratings (等级) ?

A lot of different rating bodies are considered "official" guides to hotels. But in the United States, the three most-trusted are AAA, Forbes, and Michelin.

AAA: To get AAA-approved，a hotel must pass an exhaustive (详尽的) 33-point checklist designed to ensure that the travel agency is not recommending an establishment where you'll contract (感染) ringworm (癣病). The criteria aren't unreasonable, and could apply pretty easily to a Motel 6. Once a property has been AAA-approved, it then can apply for the vaunted (值得夸耀的) AAA One-Five Diamond Ratings. These are based on 77 categories, with a specific criteria set for each level of star.

In order to receive Five Diamonds, rooms must not only be clean and luxurious, but include specialized design features, valet dry cleaning (代客干洗), 24-hour reception, separate enclosed areas for the toilet, sheets with over 400 thread count (织物经纬密度), legitimate (合法的) artwork on the walls, and some sort of decorative ceiling, among other things. The entire process is laid out in a 41-page guide that you can study before bed tonight. The main problem with the Diamond system, though, is that it requires the property to provide televisions in the rooms and a swimming pool just to get about Three Diamonds. And while exceptions are made — like for the pool-less Plaza in New York — many high-end hotels that think guests should do things other than watch TV on vacation get left, like Taylor Swift, without a Diamond.

Forbes: Forbes inspects around 1,000 hotels a year and awards only Four and Five Star ratings based on a titanic (巨大的), 800-item checklist that covers everything from the hotel to the restaurant to the spa. We'll save you the trouble of reading it and just tell you this — the criteria are derived from an algorithm (算法) built around a 70/30 service facility orientation and are the only inspection body who stays anonymously (以匿名的方式). That said, Forbes' guide is available online at ForbesTravelGuide.com totally free, and is more comprehensive than the AAA system.

Michelin: Michelin, whose Red Guide was once upon a time the hotel bible for travelers, is now more known for its ranking of chefs and restaurants. So while a culinary (烹饪的) establishment

that can boast a star from the big fat tire man is considered one of the best in the world, its rankings for hotels aren't quite as comprehensive. Yes, if you head over to the Michelin travel site, you will find star rankings for hotels. And, yes, that hotel could legitimately say it's a "3-star Michelin hotel." But, to be honest, that ranking isn't a whole lot more meaningful than one you'd find on a comparable travel site.

What about Online Star Ratings?

Other outlets (出路) offer star systems too, of course, the most common of which you'll find on travel booking sites like TripAdvisor, Expedia, and HotWire. These sites have absolutely NO standardized criteria for what qualifies as one-five stars, and unless they're user-generated, you won't have any idea what level of room you're really booking. Each site, however, does provide a basic description of what its star systems mean, and most definitions are pretty similar. Just to repeat: those classifications are not based on a set criteria like Forbes, AAA, or Michelin.

Many countries allow various classification systems for hotels in accordance to chain name and type of hotel; however, there is no international classification which has been adopted. There have been attempts at unifying the classification system so that it becomes an internationally recognized and reliable standard but large differences exist in the quality of the accommodation and the size and design of the accommodation. Food services, entertainment, view, room variations such as size and additional amenities (服务设施), spas and fitness centers and location are also vital in establishing a standard. As a rough guide:

One-star hotels: Here, there are only basic room options available. In the UK, five letting bedrooms must be available to qualify. The hotel must also be open seven days per week during its operating season and staff must be available during the day to receive and check-in guests. Occasionally, bathroom facilities will be shared and there will likely not be any sort of restaurant or bar on-site. However, there will usually be vending machines.

Two-star hotels: While room options will likely still be basic at these properties, there will usually be television and phone in the room, as well as private en-suite bathrooms (套间浴室) and an in-house bar or restaurant. There will also be higher levels of cleanliness, maintenance and services delivered that the hotel must maintain.

Three-star hotels: There will almost definitely be several different categories of room available in these hotels, as well as a restaurant, basic gym facilities and a conference room or business centre available. In the UK, to qualify as a three-star hotel, residents must have access to the property at all times during the day and evening, without use of a key. Room service must also be available and wifi must be offered in public areas. All rooms will include en-suite bathrooms and an internal telephone system for guests to reach reception.

Four-star hotels: Here, the expectation for higher quality level of service is the standard across all departments. Higher staffing levels are also expected. There will be several room options available, including suites. There may also be several restaurants and bars on site, extensive business facilities, concierge (前台服务) services and a swimming pool and gym. In the UK, residents must have 24-hour access to the hotel and must always be met by on-duty staff. Additionally, 24-hour room service must be offered, as well as enhanced food and beverage options. Wifi, or another internet connection, will be provided in all bedrooms and all en-suite bathrooms must contain a thermostatically-controlled (温控) shower.

Five-star hotels: At a five-star property, accommodations will boast all of the facilities included in a four-star hotel, as well as excellent staff with exceptional levels of proactive (积极主动的) service and customer care. Cleanliness, maintenance, hospitality and delivery of services must all adhere to an extremely high standard. In the UK, the hotel must also offer extensive fitness and spa facilities, valet parking (代客停车), butler services (管家服务), concierge services (礼宾服

务), 24-hour reception and room service, and a full afternoon tea. There must also be a choice of environments in public areas of sufficient size to provide generous personal space for guests. Additionally, at least one permanent suite — comprised of three separate rooms: a bedroom, lounge (客厅) and bathroom — must always be available to rent.

What about in Europe?

Europeans established a trans-European organization called HOTREC. Formed in 2004, it has standardized hotel star ratings in 20 countries, including all of the ones you'd probably want to go

to except England. The UK has its own version of AAA, called the AA, which rates hotels. No word on if it also offers encouraging weekly meetings with free coffee. The European HOTREC criteria can be found here. They are far more stripped down and generalized than the AAA-Diamond system, as a nice hotel doesn't need much more than a personal greeting and flowers in the room to rate five stars. Clearly, it doesn't get as carried away with complimentary (免费的) lavender bubble bath (薰衣草泡泡浴) as Americans do.

What about Those Seven- and Eight-star Hotels?

You might have heard about the Burj-al-Arab (阿拉伯高塔酒店) in Dubai, dubbed (授予称号) by some as the world's first eight-star hotel. Who are "some" you ask? Mostly online reviewers and bloggers who love hyperbole (夸张). Not even self-promotion-obsessed Dubai has attempted to use seven- and eight-star ratings as marketing strategies. As of now, NO rating body — not Forbes, not AAA, not any trade agency like Europe's HOTREC — awards more than five stars. So don't buy into the hype (炒作), because it's all a

big gimmick (噱头).

What about the Rest of the World?

For the record, there is no worldwide system of star classification; if you can't find it rated by either a governing body or a standardized rating agency, the star claims are probably not much more than marketing. Then again, guesswork is half the fun of travel just as long as you guess right.

I. Choose the best choice to answer or finish each of the following questions.

1. The author's purpose in writing this passage is to _____.

   A. offer some information about the construction of hotels

   B. make advertisements for some renowned hotels

   C. explain how the starred hotels are managed

   D. introduce how the starred hotels are rated

2. According to the AAA standard, the room of a 3-starred hotel has to contain a _____.

   A. radio   B. television

C. air conditioner   D. wifi service

3. Compared with the AAA system, Forbes ratings are more _____.

A. general   B. simple

C. complicated   D. advanced

4. Michelin rankings are now famous for the ranking of _____.

A. foods   B. hotels   C. cars   D. tires

5. What is the author's attitude towards ranking systems other than AAA, Forbes and Michelin?

A. Favorable.   B. Doubtful.

C. Opposing.   D. Neutral.

II. Match the words or phrases with their definitions.

WORDS OR PHRASES	DEFINITIONS
1. assign	A. to make an official visit to a building, organization etc. to check whether everything is satisfactory
2. establishment	B. to give a particular standard to value something
3. inspect	C. an organization or institution, especially a business, shop etc.
4. reliable	D. to remove detachable parts so as to make something brief
5. strip down	E. someone or something that can be trusted or depended on

III. Decide whether the following statements are true or false according to Passage III.

1. The online 5-star standard of hotel classification is internationally recognized. (   )

2. The ranking of hotels cannot be unified because there are too many changing factors. (   )

3. Generally speaking, there might be no receptionist available in the 1-star hotels. (   )

4. According to the passage, there should be internet service in all the rooms of 3-star hotels. (   )

5. Roughly speaking, a restaurant attached to the hotel is required only for the hotels above 3 stars. (   )

6. The AAA hotel rating system is also applied in England. (   )

7. The hotel rating system in Europe is less specific than it is in USA. (   )

8. Burj-al-Arab Hotel in Dubai is a 7-star hotel according to Forbes ranking system. (   )

9. The highest rating of hotels in the world is 5-star. (   )

10. Some hotels may have a star claim without any approval. (   )

Unit 5

Travel

Lead-in

We all know travelling gives us lots of joy, experience and adventures. Traveling expands your appreciation for other people and cultures. It helps you discover more about yourself and your traveling companions. Everyone likes to travel, but everybody does it in different ways. It depends on many things such as money, time, health and other things. Mainly travels are of long and short distances. Travel is wonderful, no matter what form it takes. The form that best suits you is the best way to travel.

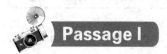

Passage I

Backpacking (背包旅游)

Think Before Reading

1. Which way of traveling do you prefer?
2. What are the characteristics of backpacking?
3. What caused the changes in backpacking nowadays?

Backpacking is a form of low-cost, independent travel. It includes the use of a backpack that is easily carried for long distances or long periods of time, the use of public transport, inexpensive lodging such as youth hostels (青年旅舍), often a longer duration of the trip when compared with conventional vacations, and typically an interest in meeting locals as well as seeing sights.

Backpacking may include wilderness adventures, local travel and travel to nearby countries while working from the country in which they are based. The definition of a backpacker has evolved (进化) as travelers from different cultures and regions participate in the trend. A 2007 paper says "backpackers constituted (由······组成) a heterogeneous (异类的) group with respect to the diversity of rationales (理由) and meanings attached to their travel experiences. They also displayed a common commitment to a non-institutionalized form of travel, which was central to their self-identification as backpackers". Backpacking, as a lifestyle and as a business, has grown

considerably in the 2000s due to low-cost airlines and hostels or budget (预算) accommodations in many parts of the world.

Visa laws in many countries such as Ireland, Australia, Canada, New Zealand and the United Kingdom enable backpackers with restricted visas to work and support themselves while they are in those countries. This allows these backpackers to earn an income while traveling in order to financially support their travels.

Over the past few decades, backpackers have traveled to South East Asia in large numbers which has caused popular Thai islands and several previously sleepy towns in Thailand, Cambodia (柬埔寨), and Laos to be transformed by the influx (涌入) of travelers. Backpacking in Europe, South America, Central America, Australia and New Zealand has also become more popular and there are several well-trodden routes (常走的路线) around the world that backpackers tend to stick to.

Technological developments and improvements have contributed to changes in backpacking. Traditionally, backpackers did not travel with expensive electronic equipment like laptop computers, digital cameras, and cell phones because of concerns about theft, damage, and additional luggage weight. However, the desire to stay connected, coupled with breakthroughs in lightweight electronics, has given rise to a trend that has been termed "flash packing".

Backpackers have traditionally carried their possessions in 30 litre to 60 litre backpacks, but roller-wheeled suitcases and some less-traditional carrying methods have become more common, and there has been a trend towards keeping pack weights under the 7 kg carry-on limit of most airlines.

Of importance to some backpackers is a sense of authenticity (真实性). Backpacking is perceived as being more than a holiday, but a means of education. Backpackers want to experience the "real" destination rather than the packaged version (打包旅游) often associated with mass tourism, which has led to the assertion (主张) that backpackers are anti-tourist. For many young people in Northern Europe, Australia, New Zealand, and Israel, backpacking is a rite of passage. In Canada, it is quite common for gap-year (空挡年) students to visit Europe. Backpackers are less commonly from China, India, the United States, Japan, and South Korea, due particularly to their large populations, accounted for by visa restrictions; yet, it is also gradually becoming more popular among rich people from those countries. Backpacking trips were traditionally undertaken either in a "gap year" between high school and university, or between the latter and the commencement (开始) of work. However, the average age of backpackers has gradually increased over time, and it is now more common to see people in their

30s, 40s, and even older to backpack during an extended career break. Some retirees enjoy backpacking.

Backpacking has been criticized, with some criticism dating back to travelers' behavior along the Hippie Trail. For example, the host countries and other travelers may disagree with the actions of backpackers. However, the perception (看法) of backpackers seems to have improved as backpacking has become more mainstream (主流). Another criticism is that even though one of the primary aims of backpacking is to seek the "authentic," the majority of backpackers spend most of their time interacting with other backpackers, and interactions with locals are of "secondary importance".

Planning and research can be an important part of backpacking, aided by such guides from companies like Lonely Planet and Rough Guides, books by travel authors such as Rick Steves, and various digital and online resources such as Wikivoyage. Resources provide information about such topics as the language, culture, food, and history. They also provide listings of accommodation and places to eat, together with maps of key locations. Digital format (电子版) guidebooks are becoming more popular, especially since the advent (出现) of smart phones and lightweight netbooks and laptops.

I. Choose the best choice to answer or finish each of the following questions.

1. Which one of the following statements is one of the features of backpacking?

   A. The backpackers usually have very small backpacks with them.

   B. Backpacking usually covers a very long duration of travelling.

   C. Backpacking often involves the use of shared bicycles.

   D. The backpackers often travel in groups.

2. Backpacking is becoming more and more popular in the world because _____.

   A. it's more and more cheap

   B. it's fashionable for the young

   C. there's no visa restrictions any more

   D. transportation is more convenient

3. Backpackers do not like to be tourists because _____.

   A. they have more withdrawn personalities

   B. they do not want to be restricted by the tourist guides

    C. they want to experience more in the process of travelling

    D. they are not willing to spend much money

4. Backpacking was criticized in some countries because _____.

    A. the local residents cannot get any profit from them

    B. most people cannot accept this way of travelling

    C. some backpackers do have some bad behaviors

    D. it is quite dangerous to travel as a backpacker

5. The most popular sources of information for the backpackers are from _____.

    A. the local residents they meet on the way

    B. paper books written by famous travellers

    C. the Association of Backpackers

    D. electronic versions of resources

II. Match the words with their definitions.

WORDS	DEFINITIONS
1. duration	A. arrival of people
2. influx	B. the period of time during which something continues
3. contribute	C. the time at which something is supposed to begin
4. perceive	D. to become aware of through the senses
5. commencement	E. to provide

III. Fill in the blanks in following passage with words from Passage I.

    Backpacking is a form of travel which is popular due to its 1_____ transportation and accommodations in many parts of the world. Backpackers usually regard travelling as a means of 2_____ because they want to experience "real" destinations. However, backpacking has been 3_____ because of two reasons which include the bad actions of backpackers as well as their fewer interactions with the locals. Planning and research can be an important part of backpacking, and the main information resources of backpacking are various 4_____ and online resources providing information about such topics as the language, culture, food, and history. They also provide 5_____ of accommodation and places to eat, together with maps of key locations.

Passage II

In Mexico City Pleasantries (客气话) Help Keep the City Afloat

Think Before Reading

1. Why do people think "He who get angry, loses" in Mexico City?

2. What benefits can you get if you speak pleasantries?

3. Do you know anything about the history of colonization in Mexico?

I'd lived in Mexico City for about six months before witnessing somebody get visibly angry in public. And it wasn't a Mexican.

It was just after the workday had ended, and the buzzing (嗡嗡响) cafe I was in had a perpetual (永久的) line wrapped around the counter. Suddenly a man began to raise his voice toward the cashier. "You're trying to rob me!" he yelled in Spanish, with a non-Mexican accent.

He looked around the cafe and announced loudly that he had given the cashier 500 pesos, but had only received change for 200 pesos. The young cashier appeared mortified (窘迫的), and people in line turned their gaze to their feet or the pastry (糕点) display in front of them.

"This is unbelievable!" The man was now shouting, his anger and frustration directed at everyone in the cafe. "This is criminal."

No-one came to his aid. Everyone was simply too shocked that he would raise his voice so aggressively. Finally, the cashier turned around and went into the back room. The man *huffed and puffed* (恼怒) for another minute before storming out of the establishment. Once he was out of

sight, the cashier returned, smiled at the next customer and continued taking orders as usual. I have no idea where this man was from, but clearly, he wasn't from Mexico City, or Mexico anywhere. Rarely will you see a Mexican publicly lose emotional control, unless perhaps an excess of tequila (龙舌兰酒) has been involved.

This is because there are two things that will get you absolutely nowhere in Mexico: getting visibly upset and being overly direct.

From a young age, Mexicans are taught not to get overly emotional. The common Mexican saying is "He who gets angry, loses."

"We're taught that we need to remain as calm as possible in every situation," said Eleazar Silvestre, a fellow Mexico City transplant (移居者) who is originally from the northern desert state of Sonora.

And this is taken to a whole new level in the central part of the country, including Mexico City, which is considered one of Latin America's most modern and cosmopolitan (大都市) cities.

"You cannot be direct here, under any circumstances," Silvestre said.

The cultural norms in Mexico City involve a level of politeness, at least on a superficial level, that I've not experienced in other cities of its size. Surely, with 25 million people making their way through the sprawling megalopolis (特大城市) daily, tensions should be remarkably high. But here, there's a sort of organized chaos (混乱) and functionality resting on exchanges of pleasantries (routine greetings and farewells specifically, especially among strangers) and an impressive level of

patience. Two things that will get you absolutely nowhere in Mexico: getting visibly upset and being overly direct.

For example, a simple request of "please pass the salt" goes down much better in Mexico City if worded as "Could you please pass me the salt if you would be so kind" and followed by a "How kind. Thank you very much."

These traditions of respectful language have been handed down by the country's indigenous (本土的) populations (including the Aztecs, whose descendants are the modern day Nahuas), later blending with the courtly traditions of the Spanish when Hernán Cortés and his team of conquistadors (西班牙征服者) marauded (掠夺) through the region in 1519. While the north of the country was settled very differently, with a less distinct colonial period, central and southern Mexico were heavily influenced by 300 years of Spanish rule followed by nearly 100 years of Mexican dictatorships.

In some indigenous communities, including some Nahua communities, not looking people in the eye while speaking to them is a sign of respect, while holding eye contact for a prolonged period, especially when done between two men, can be seen as a symbol of aggression.

The poor treatment of indigenous people over the course of the country's history is a sensitive topic in Mexico City, and the influences of the past can still be seen today in the country's social structure and indirect communication style. In some ways, it's a lack of desire to rock the boat (破坏现状) any further, in a country where people have a serious distrust in any authority. Politeness in Mexico City specifically is a form of setting up a barrier between oneself and the outside world. That combined with a sincere desire to not upset anyone. For example, if you've ever asked for directions in Mexico City, you may have found yourself wandering in circles as you follow the instructions of someone who didn't want to seem rude by confessing they had no idea where to direct you.

Similarly, when in a taxi, including a politeness ritual that extends beyond a simple greeting will find you enjoying a much smoother, more pleasant and perhaps even less-expensive ride. Start barking orders thanklessly, whether to your barista (咖啡师) or a parking attendant, and you'll come up against unthinkably old resentments (愤恨). For example, if you do not overextend yourself in your greeting, or are bossy, rude or selfish, you may be seen as being not unlike a conquistador.

It's not to say that everyone in Mexico City is "nice". But for one of the most densely populated cities in the world with many problems (from crime to water scarcity, corruption to traffic), many travelers find themselves remarking that at least here, people take the time for pleasantries. They help keep the city afloat. And that's important in a city built on an ancient lake bed, with parts of it sinking at about 20 cm a year.

In the nearly two years I've lived in Mexico City, I've learned that maintaining this strict level of pleasantries is an art. Everyone is in it together, combing through the madness of a massive city just trying to live their lives. I'm merely one of millions. And I never skip (跳过) an opportunity to wish a stranger "good day" or to profusely (丰富地) thank someone for doing me a favor, even when I've paid for it.

I. Choose the best choice to answer or finish each of the following questions.

1. The man in the café was shouting because _____.

   A. he received less change than he expected

   B. his money was stolen by the cashier

   C. he was ill-treated by the waiter

   D. he was dissatisfied with the drink

2. What's the reaction of the customers to the incident in the café?

   A. They were indifferent to the man.

   B. They blamed the cashier openly.

   C. They showed sympathy to the man.

   D. They drove the man out of the café.

3. Which of the following statements is true about eye contact in native Mexican communities?

   A. Looking people in the eye while speaking to them is a sign of respect.

   B. Holding eye contact for a prolonged period is a sign of politeness.

   C. Holding eye contacts between two women can be seen as a symbol of aggression.

   D. Having no eye contacts is regarded as respectful while talking.

4. The author thinks there is an "organized chaos" in Mexico City because _____.

   A. its political system is well organized

   B. people speak pleasantries frequently

   C. everybody observe the law strictly

   D. wars often happen in the city

5. What's the author's attitude towards the use of pleasantries in Mexico City?

   A. It is not clearly shown.

   B. He does not like it.

   C. He is neutral to it.

   D. He is in favor of it.

II. Match the words with their definitions.

WORDS	DEFINITIONS
1. witness	A. continuing for a long time
2. aggressively	B. not often
3. rarely	C. in a forceful manner
4. prolonged	D. someone who sees an event and reports what happened
5.maintain	E. keep in a certain state, position, or activity

III. Decide whether the following statements are true or false according to Passage II.

1. The author has lived in Mexico for six months. (　　)

2. Everybody in the café showed sympathy toward the man who yelled at the cashier. (　　)

3. Mexicans regard it shameful to lose temper in public. (　　)

4. Mexicans use more pleasantries because the local tradition has been mixed with the Spanish influence. (　　)

5. Although Mexico City is very big it is peaceful with few crimes and corruption. (　　)

Passage III

Sustainable Travel: What Is It and Why Is It So Important?

Think Before Reading

1. Do you have an awareness of environmental protection when you are travelling?
2. Do you think we should protect the environment when travelling?
3. What do you know about the Indian culture?

(A) "Sustainability" is the word on everybody's lips these days. We're constantly hearing about responsible tourism, eco-lodges and waste being dumped into the ocean. The concept of "being green" has filtered (渗透) down to all of us in one way or another — but how do we ensure it doesn't become another shallow Instagram ("照片墙"，一款图片分享 App) trend? It's time we all engage seriously with the issue of sustainable travel.

What Is Sustainable Travel?

(B) Are you one of those people who occasionally feels guilty getting flying? You're not alone. When I started to think more about my own carbon footprint, one issue appeared to be so large and it ended up becoming the elephant in the room, something I couldn't keep ignoring: how could I square (调整) my passion for travel with sustainability? On the face of it, it seemed like the answer was simply "you can't". However, once I took a closer look, I discovered there are a lot of ways to solve this problem.

(C) The concept of sustainable tourism rests on three main pillars, namely: The ecological pillar, conserving the natural environment of the destination you are visiting；the economic pillar, supporting local businesses there；the social pillar, supporting cultural projects there. Here is how you can put that practice into action on your own travels.

The Ecological Pillar: Consider Your Impact on the Environment

(D) Planes are a major issue when it comes to the environment — the CO_2 emissions (排放) per-passenger are huge. So it's important to consider the length of your trip in relation to the distance you're travelling. In practice, this means the further you fly, the longer you should stay there. So if you're considering a trip to the Caribbean then you should stay for at least two weeks rather than flying there and back in a week. Another way to minimize your environmental impact on a trip is to eat less meat when travelling — and try to cut down at home too. Intensive livestock (牲畜) farming is still the number one cause of CO_2 emissions.

(E) A key sustainable travel practice (which may sound really obvious but you would be surprised how many travelers still do this), is to always take all your rubbish with you. Never ever leave anything behind on a beach or on a hiking trail — pack it away and dispose of it properly later. An easy solution is to bring your own reusable water bottle from home instead of constantly buying plastic bottles in the supermarket. Research in advance if the tap-water is safe to drink in the country you're visiting or look out for a water cooler in your hostel. It's also a good idea to take old T-shirts or broken or worn out shoes home and dispose of them there. A lot of countries just burn their rubbish instead of recycling it, which is unbelievably damaging to the environment.

(F) Another big misconception is that eco-lodges are really expensive, which is understandable given that the term is often used to beautiful luxury hotels located by sustainable beaches. Despite this, it's actually really easy to find environmentally-friendly hostel accommodation too. If the hostel is made out of wood from the rainforest, provides meals made from locally sourced ingredients and uses electricity from solar panels then you've got the makings of some really great eco-accommodation.

The Economic Pillar: Support Local Businesses

(G) First of all: the tourism industry in all its forms can boost the economy of a country, which is a great thing. However, resorts and large hotel chains with all-inclusive deals are often run from

abroad. So, if you want to directly support the local people and the economy of the country you're visiting, then avoid big hotel chains and book accommodation run by locals. The same goes for businesses: did a local fisherman offer you a tour in his own boat? Did you have a really enthusiastic and friendly local guide in the national park? Then leave them a bigger tip and recommend them to other people.

The Social Pillar: Respect the Culture and the People

(H) This section is complicated since it touches on a broad spectrum (范围) of issues: the violation (侵犯) of human rights, modern-day slavery and disrespect for cultural traditions are just

some of the things that ill-informed tourism can lead to. A lot of things go on behind closed doors that you wouldn't be aware of, so rather than feeling guilty, you should educate yourself to ensure you're better informed on your next trip. It's also important to be aware of the cultural traditions of the place you're travelling too. To start with, being generally respectful towards the people there and showing an interest in the

country is important and allows you to recognize any cultural differences or misunderstandings. Start thinking about the country you're visiting and the people who live there as you plan your trip.

India: the Perfect Destination

(I) Let's take India as a perfect destination to illustrate the social pillar. This huge subcontinent (次大陆) has bags of surprises in store. There are incredible temples scattered across the whole country just waiting for you to visit. You'll have the chance to encounter a wide range of religions, cultural traditions and people from different backgrounds. Even though Indian people are generally very friendly, helpful and full of curiosity, the country's poverty and hygiene (卫生) standards can be a shock at first. What better place to broaden your horizons and question your assumptions while meeting with other people, leaving your preconceptions (偏见) behind you?

Respecting Other Cultures

(J) India is a very ethnically and culturally diverse country. It is home to over 100 different languages, as well as countless religions and cultures, all in one big melting-pot (熔炉). Followers of Hinduism (印度教) make up 80% of the population, meaning it's the country's largest religion, followed by Islam and other religions. In this regard, it's important to check your guidebook (or check online) before or during your trip

through each region. The subcontinent is huge, and the differences between each state are just as big. If you respect cultural practices, such as taking off your shoes before going into a temple, the country will open its doors to you.

Be Open When Meeting the Locals

(K) In India, people often stare at tourists and come up to them. It can take a little getting used to at first, but if you're willing to be open towards people you don't know, you should give it a go in India. There will be a lot of people who want to have their photo taken with you. It's even true that female tourists are often asked to hold a local baby — it's supposed to bring good luck.

Sometimes the endless attention you receive can get a bit annoying, disconcerting and tiresome. You're not a robot, so it's ok to say "no" sometimes. However, most of the time the encounters will be really interesting and allow you to get a broader view of the world. Anyway, you came here for a reason, right? To get to know another culture? So get going and do just that!

Support Social Projects in a Meaningful Way

(L) A lot of travelers really want to help, but forget that aid work is really complex. If, for example, you decide to volunteer in an Indian orphanage (孤儿), you won't realize until you're leaving how difficult it is for the children to see you go. The emotional bonds they form are ripped (撕裂) apart, again and again. So, what else can you do to help out? Well, one way is supporting social infrastructure (基础设施) through responsible consumption, which is something you can easily do at home too. The German label "Glimpse Clothing" offers Indian women somewhere safe

to work and rescues them from the spiral (旋涡) of violence. Another piece of advice: before visiting a region, approach a couple of local aid organizations and ask if there is a need for any specific aid goods (e.g. pens, books, chalk) so bring a few useful products with you.

(M) The ability to travel the world in a sustainable way lies with us. It's not always just about having fun, but isn't that part of the experience of travelling? To get a

broader view of the world and a glimpse what really lies beneath the surface? In twenty years' time, don't we still want the experience of travelling to be the same as we imagine now? Standing by a clear mountain lakes and walking along spotless beaches? Encountering other cultures and learning new things now and again? If your answer is YES, then we'll have to choose to travel in a way that is sustainable and responsible now. The reality is, it's not that hard. We just have to make a start.

I. Choose the best choice to answer or finish each of the following questions.

1. In order to reduce the CO_2 emission, the author suggests _____.

   A. giving up traveling on air

   B. spending more time on vacations

   C. eating no meat when travelling

   D. reducing the consumption of meat

2. Eco-accommodation in travelling may not involve _____.

   A. staying in a luxury hotel by sustainable beaches

   B. using electricity generated from coals and petrol

   C. having meals made from locally sourced ingredients

   D. staying in a hostel made out of wood from the rainforest

3. The author suggests choosing local hotels and guides because _____.

   A. it helps to develop the local economy

   B. it makes you feel more involved in local culture

   C. it is less dangerous

   D. it is less expensive

4. Which of the following deed is proper to support Indian social projects?

   A. Volunteering in an Indian orphanage.

   B. Investing on the construction of local buildings.

   C. Donating some old clothes to the local people.

   D. Offering some jobs to the India women.

5. According to the passage, what is the purpose of sustainable travel?

   A. To find some hidden social and political truth.

   B. To help in improving the world economy.

   C. To save the people in poor countries by making donations.

   D. To learn different cultures by protecting the environment.

II. Match the words with their definitions.

WORDS	DEFINITIONS
1. sustainable	A. a fundamental principle or practice
2. ecological	B. to make somebody free from harm or evil
3. ingredient	C. able to continue without causing damage to the environment
4. pillar	D. connected with the way plants, animals and people are related to each other and to their environment
5. rescue	E. food that is used to make a dish

III. Identify the paragraph from which the information is derived.

_____ 1. We should respect the local culture of the country we visit.

_____ 2. The meaning of sustainable travel and the 3 aspects it includes are listed in this passage.

_____ 3. India is a country full of cultural diversity.

_____ 4. It is suggested that the passengers should do some proper things to have a sustainable flight.

_____ 5. Tourists are suggested to take proper actions to help the local Indians.

_____ 6. Tourists can do many things to support the local business of the visited country.

_____ 7. Tourists should be open in communicating with the local Indians.

_____ 8. Tourists are suggested to choose to accommodate in a sustainable way.

_____ 9. Tourists should have a proper conception on the purpose of having sustainable travels.

_____ 10. Because of cultural differences, India is a perfect destination to have a sustainable travel.

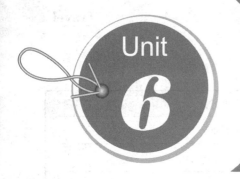

Unit 6

Transportation

 Lead-in

Transportation is a concern of every traveler, whether he is planning how to reach a destination or trying to hail (打车) a taxi. Humans' first means of transport involved walking, running and swimming. While nowadays, a majority of people rely on the modern public transportation for their daily trip, for it has brought them a great many advantages as well as convenience (便捷). However the development of the modern transportation system also causes a lot of problems, such as pollution, traffic jams and accidents. We still need to spend more money in improving public transportation because it is a key component (要素) of growth and globalization after all.

 **Passage I**

Modes of Green Transportation

We've learned that the existing modes of transportation require enormous amounts of energy. Many recognize that these very automobiles cause a lot of pollution, which impacts the environment and leads to health complications (困境). Promising innovative technologies could be the ultimate (最终的) solution, but before such innovations come to fruition (实现), the world can play a significant role by utilizing eco-friendly modes of transportation obtainable (可获得的).

Though it is much more comfortable and convenient to drive one's own private vehicle to office or market every other day but being a responsible citizen one should opt for (选择) green transportation that is easily accessible to everyone. Let's look at some of the modes of green transportation available in this age.

1. Bicycle

This is a no brainer. Using a bicycle to commute is another great mode of green transportation. Riding a bicycle instead of driving a car enormously contributes to ridding (使摆脱) the atmosphere of greenhouse gases. Although walking is a great green transportation mode, a bicycle

has far reaching benefits because it's faster, plus it's in itself a form of workout. Buying and maintenance (维护) cost is only a fraction (一小部分) of that required for a car.

2. Electric Bikes

Electric bikes are great modes of green transportation because they don't release any harmful emission (排放物) into the environment. With an electric bike, only light peddling is needed. The speed of electric bikes is greatly regulated by law, though. Some countries limit electric bike speeds at 20 mph. Still, in other countries, you must have a special registration, license, and insurance to be able to ride an electric bike.

3. Electric Vehicles

Some notable kinds of electric vehicles include cars, motorcycles, lorries, trains, and boats. Electric vehicles powered entirely by electricity do not emit any dangerous gases, even though the toxic (有毒的) emissions might be produced by plants generating the electricity. Still, the power can be tapped from renewable technologies like geothermal (地热的), hydroelectric (水力发电的), solar power and wind turbines (涡轮机).

Opting for green vehicles powered by alternative fuels and advanced vehicle technologies puts less pressure on the environment as compared to conventional internal combustion engine (内燃机) vehicles running on petrol or diesel (柴油).

4. Green Trains

With most world governments now dedicated to supporting green transportation than ever, trains are getting increasingly greener with hybrid locomotives (混合动力机车) and other innovative green technologies. The innovative hybrid locomotives utilize similar technologies applied in hybrid cars.

The modern electric trains make use of electrified third rail (供电轨), overhead lines or devices that store up energy like fuel cells. The advantage of these electric trains is that they travel at top speeds of more than 200 mph, yet maintaining high levels of safety.

5. Electric Motorcycles

Like other electric vehicles, electric motorcycles do not give off emissions. They are typically battery (蓄电池) powered. Nonetheless, pollution may occur as a result of generation of grid (电网) electricity utilized to charge electric bike batteries. Electric motorcycles, however, come with a huge price tag. The cheapest electric motorcycle could cost you about $7,000.

6. Multiple Occupant Vehicles

The explosion of vehicles around the world is due to the booming world economy. While this is a milestone many are happy about, pollution levels have significantly increased. Multiple occupant vehicles, also referred to as carpools (拼车), reduce the number of vehicles on roads, hence, minimizing levels of pollution. Multiple occupant vehicles are very eco-friendly and is a favorable mode of green transportation.

Groups of friends and colleges can use one vehicle when habitually driving in a similar direction. Instead of 5 individuals driving their own cars in the similar direction, it's a lot more economical and ecologically sensible to make use of a single car to take all of them to the destination. Definitely it is a great way to save petrol and money!

7. Service and Freight Vehicles

These kinds of vehicles attribute to about 9% of the total toxic gas emissions. Utilizing electricity and biofuels (生物燃料) instead of the regular fossil fuel sources in services and freight vehicles, administering (执行，给予) travel demands and offering lots of travel alternatives will go a long way towards aligning (使一致) the transportation sector to conform to green transportation.

8. Hybrid Cars

Hybrid cars also rely on electricity. A vast majority of hybrid cars are designed to automatically recharge their batteries by converting energy in the course of braking. Greenhouse emissions in

hybrid cars are extremely low; emissions can range from 26%–90% lower compared to standard cars. According to experts, hybrid cars cut down health-threatening emissions by over 90%. While hybrid cars contribute little to no greenhouse emissions, they lack in some areas. The batteries have some environmental impacts. This means the caustic (腐蚀性的) substances lighting up the batteries have to be carefully and well disposed of.

9. The New Hybrid Buses (Public Transportation)

Some of the best innovative green buses have already hit the market. A classic example is the Mercedes-Benz Ciatro G BlueTec Hybrid Bus, which utilizes 4 electrical wheel hub (轮轴) motors together with automotive lithium-ion (锂离子) batteries. The lithium-ion battery is regarded as the world's largest. The battery has the capacity to store up vast amounts of energy derived from a diesel generator. The bus also generates energy in the course of breaking.

10. Pedestrians (步行者)

One should prefer to walk to the school, to work and to grocery shopping etc. Walking involves zero emission of any greenhouse gas, it's free and an additional plus is it's a good form of exercise for the body.

I. Choose the best choice to answer or finish each of the following questions.

1. In the passage, the author aims to _____.
   A. tell us that automobiles is very harmful to the environment
   B. tell us the difference between conventional vehicles and new-type traffics
   C. show us the importance of using green transportation
   D. show us some modes of green transportation available in this age

2. When the author says "This is a no brainer.", he means "_____".
   A. This is a simple-minded person.
   B. This is a question with an obvious answer.
   C. This is a stupid question.
   D. This is a foolish person.

3. Which of the following statements is true according to the passage?
   A. Electric vehicles do not release any harmful emission into the environment.
   B. Electric vehicles may produce some toxic gases.
   C. Electric vehicles are powered by petrol or diesel.
   D. Electric vehicles just mean the electric cars.

4. Which of the following statements is NOT the advantage of multiple occupant vehicles?

   A. They are very environment-friendly.

   B. They are very economical.

   C. They boom the world economy.

   D. They reduce the number of vehicles on roads.

5. Which mode of green transportation can cut down health-threatening emissions to the greatest extent?

   A. Hybrid cars.   B. Hybrid buses.

   C. Pedestrians.   D. Multiple occupant vehicles.

II. Match the words with their definitions.

WORDS	DEFINITIONS
1. alternative	A. a regular journey of some distance to and from the place of work
2. dedicate	B. serving or used in place of another
3. commute	C. put into service
4. obtainable	D. give entirely to a specific person, activity, or cause
5. utilize	E. possible to get or achieve

III. Answer the following questions according to the Passage I.

1. What can people do to solve the pollution problem before the innovative technologies come to fruition?

   _____

   _____

2. What are the benefits of bicycles compared with walking?

   _____

   _____

3. How will the problem of toxic emissions produced by plants generating the electricity be solved when electric vehicles are used?

   _____

   _____

Public Transportation in Tokyo: What Every Intern (新来者) Must Know

Think Before Reading

1. Which mode of transportation would you like to choose if you arrive at a new big city?
2. Why should people know some local travel customs in Tokyo?

Tokyo is one of the busiest urban cities in the world, which prides itself in having one of the best transport systems in the world. Getting around this fast-paced mega (巨大的) city is not, as they say, "a-walk-in-the-park". Foreigners and locals alike, can easily get lost in the heavily-congested (严重拥挤的) streets and public transport stations in the city. Around 40 million people flock (群集) the city daily, causing major traffic jams on the roads and on the sidewalks, not to mention most streets which have no names making the city even more difficult to navigate (航行).

For interns traveling to Tokyo, it is best to know the various modes of transportation available to take you from point A to point B, but anyone new to the city must still be prepared to get lost a time or two. Here are some basics about public transportation in Tokyo to help you prepare and adjust for the adventure.

The Railway System: Surface Trains & Subways

Tokyo has one of the most extensive, unparalleled (无可比拟的) urban transit systems in the world. It is the primary mode of traveling from one place to another in the city, made especially popular by low costs and numerous conveniently located stations. Over eight million people use the train everyday in Tokyo, from  students and employees, to tourists and business people. Although it is the fastest means of traveling, trains are almost always overcrowded during rush hours, which typically start at about seven-thirty in the morning and peaks again around five o'clock in the afternoon. Imagine your face smushed (压碎) an inch too close to the window or your body nearly crushed (挤压) by those around you, that's how overcrowded Tokyo trains can be.

Interns should also be aware that it is common practice for women to give their seats to men who are standing, which is often not the case worldwide. However, there are "women-only" cars which provide added convenience and security for women, children, individuals with physical disabilities, and pregnant women. Pickpocketing (偷窃) becomes an easy game when so many people are squeezed into such tight quarters, so you must always keep an eye on your purse or wallet.

Public Buses

For those who want to avoid the "commuter hell" of trains, buses are a great alternative travel option. The fare is relatively affordable and there is no trouble of overcrowding. The only downside, travel time is slower compared to trains and you may have to walk a while to get to a station or take another mode of travel to get to your final destination, since bus stops are not as prevalent around the city as train stations.

Taxis

Interns who want to get to a place fast might want to take a taxi, but for those staying in Tokyo for an extended period taxis are definitely not the most efficient form of transport. Drivers in Tokyo are known to be trustworthy and never take advantage of their passengers, therefore providing

added security of passengers, especially those who are new to the country. If it is of absolute necessity to take a taxi, know that it is expensive, especially on weekends. Cost-conscious interns should seek out alternative means of travel, unless traveling in groups, when taxis can be more economical.

Taxi doors typically open and close automatically, so don't bother doing it yourself. Tipping is not customary in Japan and drivers do not accept tips. When you are worried about the difficulty of communicating an address, write it on paper or show the driver the location on a map. Better yet, taxis are equipped with GPS, so it is not hard for drivers to find the place or for them to input an address directly into their navigation systems.

Two-Wheelers & Two-Feet

Motorcycles and bikes can be an effective means of transport in the city, particularly when it comes to parking or squeezing in between cars stuck in a traffic jam. But bikes are often

discouraged because of the high levels of traffic congestion too, since it increases the dangers of traveling by bike.

When the time comes to wander the city and get to know the streets and landmarks of Tokyo's urban landscape, it is best to walk.

With a map at hand, the chance of becoming overwhelmed by the intricate (错综复杂的) city streets is lessened and the chances for discovery are great.

General Travel Customs of Tokyo

Knowing the local travel customs can reassure interns traveling around the city for the first time and make the task seem less daunting (令人畏惧的). It is best to plan ahead of time if you are going out shopping or to explore the city's nightlife; trains and buses usually end operations at midnight, so new comers must know what, where, and when alternative modes of transportation are available. Be sure to always prepare enough cash or change for fare, although prepaid rail passes are available. Transport systems, especially trains, are strict with time and schedules, but be mindful of announcements over the loudspeakers for delays occasionally. To avoid rush hour traffic, leave early; getting an early head-start of the day is better than squeezing on to an overpopulated train or navigating a crowded street. Ultimately, it is culturally best to try all modes of transportation to see which is most convenient for each situation and purpose.

I. Match the words with their definitions.

WORDS	DEFINITIONS
1. prevalent	A. an unusual, exciting or dangerous experience or journey
2. trustworthy	B. covering a large area
3. extensive	C. most frequent or common
4. navigate	D. being reliable and responsible
5. adventure	E. to find your position and the direction you need to go in

II. Decide whether the following statements are true or false according to Passage II.

1. Because most streets have no names, foreigners and locals are easier to get lost in Tokyo. (   )

2. As the primary mode of transportation of Tokyo, the train has a lot of advantages except the price. (   )

3. It is common practice for men to give their seats to women who are standing on the train. (   )

4. The bus is not as convenient as the train in Tokyo because of fewer stations. (   )

5. The taxi drivers in Tokyo will offer the passengers good services without being paid tips. (   )

III. Fill in the blanks in following passage with words from Passage II.

Knowing the local travel 1_____ can help interns relax when they choose different modes of transportation in Tokyo. The Railway System is the most 2_____ mode by its low costs and numerous conveniently located stations. However, the overcrowded Tokyo trains make pickpocketing become an easy game. Compared with trains, the buses in Tokyo are not

so 3_____ but less crowded. The taxi drivers in Tokyo are 4_____, but the taxi fare is very high. Motorcycles and bikes also can be an 5_____ means of transport. The best way to get to know the streets and landmarks is walking. In a word, you'd better try all modes of transportation to see which is most convenient for each situation and purpose.

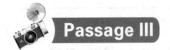

Passage III

Transport in Hong Kong

Think Before Reading

1. Can you name some types of public transport in Hong Kong?

2. Which kind of transport would you like to choose if you travel in Hong Kong?

3. Are left-hand drive cars allowed to run on the street in Hong Kong?

(A) Hong Kong has a highly developed and sophisticated (先进的) transport network, encompassing (包括) both public and private transport. Based on Hong Kong Government's Travel Characteristics Survey, over 90% of the daily journeys are on public transport, the highest rate in the world. However, in 2014 the Transport Advisory Committee, which advises the Government on transportation issues, issued a report on the much worsened congestion (拥堵) problem in Hong Kong and pointed at the excessive growth of private cars during the past 10–15 years.

(B) Hong Kong Island is dominated by steep (陡峭的), hilly terrain (地形), which required the development of unusual methods of transport up and down the slopes. In the Central and Western district, there is an extensive system of zero-fare escalators (免费自动扶梯) and moving pavements. The Mid-level Escalator (自动扶梯) is the longest outdoor covered escalator system in the world, operating downhill until 10:00 am for commuters going to work, and then operating uphill until midnight.

(C) Hong Kong has an extensive railway network, and the Hong Kong Government has long established that the public transit system has "railway as its backbone". Public transport trains are operated by the MTR Corporation Limited. Opened in 1979, the system now includes 218.2 km of rail with 161 stations, including 93 railway stations and 68 light rail stops. Nine of the lines provide general metro services, whereas the Airport Express provides a direct link from the Hong Kong International Airport into the city centre, and the Disneyland Resort Line exclusively takes passengers to and from Hong Kong Disneyland.

(D) The Hong Kong Tramways is the tram (有轨电车) system run exclusively (仅仅) with double deckers. The electric tram system was proposed in 1881; however nobody was willing to invest in a system at the time. In August 1901, the Second Tramway Bill was introduced and passed into law as the 1902 Tramway Ordinance (条例). Hong Kong Tramway Electric Company Limited, a British company, was authorized to take the responsibilities in construction and daily operation.

In 1904, the tram system first got into service. It was soon taken over by another company, Electric Transaction Company of Hong Kong Limited and then the name was changed to Hong Kong Tramways Company Limited in 1910.

(E) The Peak Tram carries both tourists and residents to the upper levels of Hong Kong Island. It provides the most direct route to Victoria Peak and offers scenic views over Victoria Harbour and the skyscrapers (摩天大楼) of Hong Kong. It was inaugurated (落成) in 1888.

(F) The Ocean Express operates within the paid area of the Ocean Park. It links two parts of the park, operating entirely in a

tunnel. The ride is themed, and uses multimedia effects to simulate the feeling of travelling into the depths of the sea. It was opened in 2009.

(G) Bus services have a long history in Hong Kong. As of 2015, five companies operate franchised (特许经营) public bus services, each granted ten-year exclusive operating rights to the set of routes that they operate. Franchised buses altogether carry about one-third of the total daily public transport market of around 12 million passengers, with KMB having 67% of the franchised bus market share, CityBus with 16% and New World First Bus with 13%. There are also a variety of non-franchised public bus services, including feeder (支线) bus services to railway stations operated by the railway companies, and residents' services for residential area (particularly those in the New Territories).

(H) Public light buses (小巴) [widely referred to as minibuses, or sometimes maxicabs (专线 小巴)] run the length and breadth of Hong Kong, through areas which the standard bus lines can not or do not reach as frequently, quickly or directly. Minibuses carry a maximum of 16 (19 for some routes since 2017) passengers; standing is not permitted.

(I) As of March 2016, there were 18,138 taxis in Hong Kong, operating in three distinct geographical areas, and distinguished by their colors. Of these, 15,250 are red urban taxis, 2,838 green New Territories taxis, and 50 blue Lantau taxis. Every day, they serve 1,400 passengers respectively. Taxis carry an average of 1 million passengers each day, occupying about 12% of the daily patronage (惠顾) carried by all modes of public transport in Hong Kong.

(J) Taxi fares are charged according to the taximeter (计价器); however, additional charges on the fare table may apply, such as road tolls and luggage fees. Urban taxis are the most expensive, while Lantau taxis are the cheapest. The standard of service among different kinds of taxis is mostly the same. The reason for having three types of taxis is to ensure service availability in less populated regions, as running in the urban centre is considered to be more profitable.

(K) As of May 2015, the Census and Statistics Department of Hong Kong reports that there are 504,798 licensed vehicles in Hong Kong. In terms of private car ownership, the number of cars per capita is half that of Singapore and one-third that of Taiwan.

However, the Transport Advisory Committee, which advises the government on transport policies, issued a report stating that the growth of private cars is too fast and must be contained so as to alleviate (减轻) congestion problems of Hong Kong.

(L) Most cars are right-hand drive models, from Japanese or European manufacturers. Hong Kong does not allow left-hand drive vehicles to be primarily registered in Hong Kong. However, Hong Kong registered vehicles may apply for secondary mainland Chinese registration plates (牌照), and these can be driven across the border to mainland China; likewise, left-hand drive cars seen in Hong Kong are usually primarily registered in mainland China and carry supplementary Hong Kong registration plates. In addition to the heavy traffic at times, parking may be problematic. Due to high urban density, there are not many filling stations; Petrol in Hong Kong averages around US$2.04 per litre, of which over half the cost is taxes.

(M) Cycling is a popular means of transport in many parts of the New Territories, where new towns such as Shatin, Tai Po and Sheung Shui have significant cycle track networks. In the auto congested urban areas of Hong Kong and Kowloon, cycling is less common, despite the relatively flat topography (地形) of populated areas, in part because it is government policy not to support cycling as part of the transportation system. In 2011, MTR Corporation announced that bicycles were permitted to be taken on all MTR rail lines.

I. Choose the best choice to answer or finish each of the following questions.

1. What is the main reason for the congestion problem in Hong Kong?

    A. The steep and hilly terrain.　　　　　B. The excessive growth of private cars.

    C. The less extensive railway network.　　D. The less common cycling.

2. The unusual method of transport in Hong Kong is _____.

    A. moving pavements　　　　　　　　B. double deckers

    C. minibuses　　　　　　　　　　　　D. trams

3. _____ provides the most direct route to Victoria Peak of Hong Kong.

    A. The Airport Express　　　　　　　B. The Ocean Express

    C. The Peak Tram　　　　　　　　　　D. The Mid-level Escalator

4. Which company shares the most franchised bus market?

   A. Hong Kong Tramways Company Limited.

   B. New World First Bus.

   C. CityBus.

   D. KMB.

5. Which is NOT the color of taxis in Hong Kong?

   A. Red.   B. Green.   C. Blue.   D. Yellow.

II. Match the words with their definitions.

WORDS	DEFINITIONS
1. congestion	A. the activity or work done in an area of business or industry
2. extensive	B. the state of being crowded and full of traffic
3. operation	C. clearly different or of a different kind
4. distinct	D. to record sb's/sth's name on an official list
5. register	E. covering a large area; great in amount

III. Identify the paragraph from which the information is derived.

_____ 1. Railway has been established as the main mode of public transit system.

_____ 2. Multimedia enables the passengers in the Ocean Express to feel the deep sea travel.

_____ 3. Passengers can choose public light buses if they run directly to a place which the standard bus line can not reach.

_____ 4. The Mid-level Escalator operates in different schedules for going downhill and uphill.

_____ 5. The left-hand drive cars in mainland China are allowed to run in Hong Kong with supplementary registration plates.

_____ 6. Cycling is less common in Kowloon because the government doesn't support it.

_____ 7. Hong Kong enjoys the highest rate of public transport occupation.

_____ 8. Paying more taxi fares than that on the fare table is possible in Hong Kong.

_____ 9. New World First Bus has the least share of the franchised bus market.

_____ 10. All the trams in Hong Kong are double deckers.

Unit 7

Entertainment

Lead-in

Entertainment has long since been observed and the forms of entertainment since then has evolved (演变). Entertainment is a form of activity or event that gives delight and pleasure capturing (引起) the interest and attention of an audience. Men may not be sane (心智健全的) without entertainment. Entertainment entertains (使快乐) us and gives us an emotion to feel. It can even motivate or inspire us. There are different types of entertainment and we all have our preferences. All however, has the same intention of capturing the spectator's attention and giving pleasure.

Passage I

Dance

Think Before Reading

1. Do you enjoy dancing in your spare time?
2. What are the factors which will influence the development of dance?
3. Can you name some types of dance in the world?

The many forms of dance provide entertainment for all age groups and cultures. Dance can be serious in tone, such as when it is used to express a culture's history or important stories; it may be

provocative (刺激的); or it may put in the service of comedy. Since it combines many forms of entertainment — music, movement, storytelling, theatre — it provides a good example of the various ways that these forms can be combined to create entertainment for different purposes and audiences.

Dance is a form of cultural representation that involves not just dancers, but choreographers (编舞者), audience members, patrons (赞助者) and impresarios (导演) coming from all over the globe and from vastly varied time periods. Whether from Africa, Asia or Europe, dance is constantly negotiating (超越) the realms (领域) of political, social, spiritual and artistic influence. Even though dance traditions may be limited to one cultural group, they all develop. For example, in Africa, there are Dahomean dances, Hausa dances, Masai dances and so forth. Ballet is an example of a highly developed Western form of dance that moved to the theatres from the French court

during the time of Louis XIV, the dancers becoming professional theatrical performers. Some dances, such as the quadrille, a square dance (方块舞) that emerged during the Napoleonic (拿破仑的) years in France and other country dances were once popular at social gatherings like balls, but are now rarely performed. On the other hand, many folk dances (such as Scottish Highland dancing and Irish dancing), have evolved into competitions, which by adding to their audiences, have increased their entertainment value. Irish dance theatre, which sometimes features traditional Irish steps and music, has developed into a major dance form with an international reputation.

Since dance is often associated with the female body and women's experiences, female dancers, who dance to entertain, have in some cases been regarded as distinct (不同) from "decent" (正派的) women because they use their bodies to make a living instead of hiding them as much as possible. Society's attitudes to female dancers depend on the culture, its history and the entertainment industry itself. For example, while some cultures regard any dancing by women as "the most shameful form of entertainment", other cultures have established venues (场所) such as strip clubs where striptease (脱衣舞) is performed in public by professional women dancers for mostly male audiences.

Various political regimes (政权) have sought to control or ban (禁止) dancing or specific types of dancing, sometimes because of disapproval of the music or clothes associated with it. Nationalism, authoritarianism (独裁主义) and racism have played a part in banning dances or dancing. For example, during the Nazi (纳粹) regime, American dances such as swing (旋转舞), regarded as "completely un-German", had become a public offense and needed to be banned. Banning had the effect of making "the dance craze (狂热)" even greater. In Ireland, the Public Dance Hall Act of 1935 banned — but did not stop — dancing at the crossroads and other popular dance forms such as house and barn dances. In the US, various dances were once banned, either because, like burlesque (滑稽表演), they were suggestive, or because, like the Twist (扭摆舞), they were associated with African Americans. African American dancers were typically banned from performing in minstrel (吟游艺人) shows until after the Civil War.

Dances can be performed solo, in pairs, in groups, or by massed performers. They might be improvised (即兴的) or highly choreographed (编排的), spontaneous (自发的) for personal entertainment, (such as when children begin dancing for themselves), a private audience, a paying audience, a world audience, or an audience interested in a particular dance genre (种类). They might

be a part of a celebration, such as a wedding or New Year, or a cultural ritual with a specific purpose, such as a dance by warriors like a haka. Some dances, such as traditional dance and ballet, need a very high level of skill and training; others, such as the can-can, require a very high level of energy and physical fitness. Entertaining the audience is a normal part of dance but its physicality (肉体) often also produces joy for the dancers themselves.

I. Choose the best choice to answer or finish each of the following questions.

1. According to the author, dance _____.

  A. provides entertainment for some particular age groups and cultures

  B. is a form of cultural representation that involves just dancers

  C. is provocative when it is used to express a culture's history or important stories

  D. proves that different forms of entertainment can be combined to entertain different audiences

2. The author lists different dances in Africa in Paragraph 2 in order to prove that _____.

  A. the highly developed western forms of dance have moved to the theatres

  B. all dance traditions have developed although they may be limited to one cultural group

  C. some dances are now rarely performed

  D. many folk dances have evolved into competitions

3. Which of the following statements about female dancers is NOT true?

  A. They are not regarded as decent women in some cases.

  B. They have been regarded as being distinct in all the cases.

  C. They should not use their bodies to make a living in some attitudes.

  D. They should hide their bodies in some attitudes.

4. The example of American swing dance being banned during the Nazi regime shows that _____.

  A. authoritarianism played a part in banning dances

  B. nationalism played a part in banning dances

  C. racism played a part in banning dances

  D. patriotism played a part in banning dances

5. Which of the following is NOT the function of dance according to the last paragraph?

  A. For personal entertainment.   B. For celebration.

  C. For high level of skill.   D. For cultural ritual.

II. Match the words with their definitions.

WORDS	DEFINITIONS
1. professional	A. put or add together
2. combine	B. undergo development
3. distinct	C. relating to a person's work
4. realm	D. not alike
5. evolve	E. an area of activity, interest, or knowledge

III. Answer the following questions according to Passage I.

1. What is the example to show that dance is negotiating the realms of social influence?

_____

_____

2. What does the author try to prove by mentioning the Public Dance Hall Act of 1935?

_____

_____

3. What is the real meaning of dance according to the last paragraph?

_____

_____

_____

Passage II

Film Industry

Think Before Reading

1. Can you name some famous film companies in the world?
2. What are the common institutions of filmmaking?

    The film industry or motion picture industry comprises (由······组成) the technological and commercial institutions of filmmaking, i.e., film production companies, film studios, cinematography (电影摄制艺术), animation (动画片制作), film production, screenwriting, pre-production, post production, film festivals, distribution (分销); and actors, film directors, and other film crew personnel.

Though the expense involved in making films almost immediately led film production to concentrate under the auspices (支持) of standing production companies, advances in affordable film making equipment, and expansion of opportunities to acquire investment capital from outside the film industry itself, have allowed independent film production to evolve. Hollywood is the oldest film industry of the world, and the largest in terms of box office gross revenue (收入). Indian cinema (including Bollywood) is the largest film industry in terms of the number of films produced and the number of tickets sold, with 3.5 billion tickets sold worldwide annually (compared to Hollywood's 2.6 billion tickets sold annually) and 1,986 feature films (剧情片) produced annually.

The worldwide theatrical market had a box office (票房收入) of US$38.6 billion in 2016. The top three regions by box office gross were: Asia-Pacific with US$14.9 billion, the United States and Canada with US$11.4 billion, and Europe, the Middle East and North Africa with US$9.5 billion. As of 2016, the largest markets by box office were, in decreasing order, the United States, China, Japan, India, and the United Kingdom. As of 2011, the countries with the largest number of film productions were India, Nigeria, and the United States. In Europe, significant centers of movie production are France, Germany, Italy, Spain, and the United Kingdom.

The cinema of the United States, often generally referred to as Hollywood, has had a profound effect on cinema across the world since the early 20th century. The United States cinema (Hollywood) is the oldest film industry in the world which originated more than 121 years ago and also the largest film industry in terms of revenue. Hollywood is the primary nexus (纽带) of the US film industry with established film study facilities such as the American Film Institute, LA Film School and NYFA being established in the area. However, four of the six major film studios are owned by East Coast companies. The

major film studios of Hollywood including Metro-Goldwyn-Mayer, 20th Century Fox, Paramount Pictures and Lightstorm Entertainment are the primary source of the most commercially successful movies in the world, such as *Gone with the Wind* (1939), *Star Wars* (1977), and *Titanic* (1997). American film studios today collectively generate several hundred movies every year, making the United States one of the most prolific (多产的) producers of films in the world.

The cinema of China, including the cinema of Hong Kong and the cinema of Taiwan, is one of three distinct historical threads of Chinese-language cinema. Cinema was introduced into China in 1896 and the first Chinese film, *The Battle of Dingjunshan*, was made in 1905, with the film industry being centered in Shanghai in the first decade. China is the home of the largest film studio in the world, the Hengdian World Studios, and in 2010 it had the third largest film industry by number of feature films produced annually. In 2012 the country became the second-largest market in the world by box office receipts (收入). In 2014, the gross box office (票房总收入) in China was US$4.82 billion, with domestic films having a share of 55%. The country is predicted to have the largest market in the world in 2017 or 2018.

India is the largest producer of films in the world and second oldest film industry in the world which originated around about 105 years ago. In 2009 India produced a total of 2,961 films on celluloid (胶片); this figure includes 1,288 feature films. Besides being the largest producer of films in the world, India also has the largest number of admissions (入场券). Indian film industry is multi-lingual (多语言的) and the largest in the world in terms of ticket sales but 3rd largest in terms of revenue mainly due to having almost the lowest ticket prices in the world. The industry is viewed mainly by a vast film-going Indian public, and Indian films have been gaining increasing popularity

in the rest of the world — notably in countries with large numbers of expatriate (侨民) Indians. Indian film industry is also the dominant source of movies and entertainment in its neighboring countries of South Asia. The largest film and most popular industry in India is the Hindi film industry mostly concentrated in Bombay, and is commonly referred to as Bollywood, an amalgamation (合并) of Bombay and Hollywood.

I. Match the words with their definitions.

WORDS	DEFINITIONS
1. originate	A. to bring something together in one place
2. dominant	B. to bring into being
3. concentrate	C. to set up or lay the groundwork for
4. receipt	D. more important, powerful or noticeable than other things
5. establish	E. the amount of money received during a particular period

II. Decide whether the following statements are true or false according to Passage II.

1. Hollywood is the largest film industry in terms of the number of films produced and the number of tickets sold. (   )

2. Nigeria was the country with the second largest number of film productions as of 2011. (   )

3. Hollywood owns most of the major film studios in the United States. (   )

4. Hengdian World Studios in China is the largest film studio in the world. (   )

5. Due to the low ticket prices, Indian film industry is only the third largest in terms of revenue although it is the largest in terms of ticket sales. (   )

III. Fill in the blanks in following passage with words from Passage II.

The film industry has seen considerable 1_____ in modern times. Hollywood in the United States is the oldest film industry of the world with more than121-year history, and the largest in terms of box office gross 2_____. Cinema was introduced in China in the end of 19th century and centered in Shanghai in the first 3_____. Now China has the largest film studio in the world and is 4_____ to have the largest market in the world in the future. Indian cinema is the largest film industry in terms of the number of films produced and the number of tickets sold. Bollywood, a combination of Bombay and Hollywood, is the largest film and most 5_____ industry in India.

Passage III

Talk Show

Think Before Reading

1. Do you like to watch a talk show on television?
2. What is a talk show according to your idea?
3. Can you name some major formats of talk shows?

A talk show or chat show is a television programming or radio programming genre (形式) in which one person or a group of people discusses various topics put forth by a talk show host.

Usually, guests consist of a group of people who are learned or who have great experience in relation to whatever issue is being discussed on the show for that episode (集). Other times, a single guest discusses their work or area of expertise (专业领域) with a host or co-hosts. A call-in show takes live phone calls from callers listening at home, in their cars, etc. Sometimes, guests are already seated but are often introduced and enter from backstage. There have been many notable talk show hosts; in many cases, the shows have made their hosts famous.

There are several major formats of talk shows. Generally, each subgenre (种类, 亚属) predominates (主导) during a specific programming block during the broadcast day. Breakfast chat or early morning shows that generally alternate between news summaries, political coverage, feature stories, celebrity interviews, and musical performances. Late morning chat shows feature two or more hosts or a celebrity panel, and focus on entertainment and lifestyle features. Daytime tabloid (通俗) talk shows generally feature a host, a guest or a panel of guests, and a live audience that interacts extensively with the host and guests. These shows may feature celebrities, political

commentators, or "ordinary" people who present unusual or controversial topics. "Lifestyle" or self-help programs, which generally feature a host or hosts who are medical practitioners (执业医生), therapists (治疗师), or counselors, and guests who seek intervention (干预), describe medical or psychological problems, or offer advice. Evening panel discussion shows focus on news, politics, or popular culture. Late-night talk shows feature celebrity guests who talk about their work and personal lives as well as their latest films, TV shows, music recordings, or other projects they'd like to promote to the public. The hosts are often comedians who open the shows with comedy monologues (独白). Sunday morning talk shows are a staple (产物) of network programming in North America. These shows feature elected political figures and candidates for office, commentators, and journalists. Aftershows which feature in-depth discussion about a program on the same network that aired just before (for example, Talking Dead). Spoof (恶搞) talk shows, such as *Space Ghost Coast to Coast*, where the interviews are mostly scripted, and shown in a humorous and satirical (讽刺的) way, or the show engages in subverting (颠覆) the norms of the format.

These formats are not absolute. Syndicated (联合的) "daytime" shows may appear overnight in some markets, and some afternoon programs have similar structures to late night talk shows. These formats may vary across different countries or markets. Late night talk shows are especially significant in the United States. Breakfast television is a staple of British television. The daytime talk format has become popular in Latin America as well as the United States.

Politics are hardly the only subject of American talk shows, however. Other radio talk show subjects include *Car Talk* hosted by NPR and *Coast to Coast AM* hosted by Art Bell and George Noory which discusses topics of the paranormal (超自然), conspiracy (阴谋) theories, fringe (边缘) science, and the just plain weird. Sports talk shows are also very popular ranging from high-budget shows like *The Best Damn Sports Show Period* to Max Kellerman's original public-access television cable TV show *Max on Boxing*.

Talk shows have been broadcast on television since the earliest days of the medium. Joe Franklin, an American radio and television personality, hosted the first television talk show. The show began in 1951 on WJZ-TV and moved to WOR-TV from 1962 to 1993.

NBC's *The Tonight Show* is the world's longest-running talk show; having debuted (首秀) in 1954, it continues to this day. The show underwent some minor title changes until settling on its current title in 1962, and despite a brief foray (尝试) into a more news-style program in 1957 and then reverting that same year, it has remained a talk show. Ireland's *The Late Late Show* is the second-longest running talk show in television history, and the longest running talk show in Europe, having debuted in 1962.

TV news pioneer Edward R. Murrow hosted a talk show entitled Small World in the late 1950s and since then, political TV talk shows have predominantly aired on Sunday mornings.

Talk shows have more recently started to appear on Internet radio. Also, several Internet blogs are in talk show format including *the Baugh Experience.*

The current world record for the longest talk show is held by Rabi Lamichhane from Nepal (尼泊尔) by staying on air for 62 hours from April 11 to 13, 2013 breaking the previous record set by two Ukrainians (乌克兰人) by airing the show for 52 hours in 2011.

In Japan, panel shows are very commonplace, accounting for about 30% of daytime and prime-time (黄金时段) programming on the four main television stations. Due to language and cultural differences, Japanese TV stations could not freely use syndicated programs (mostly from Europe and North America) and therefore turned to panel shows, which could be produced cheaply and easily, to fill time during daytime programming.

Japanese panel shows are distinct in generally not employing regular panelists but instead having a panel made up of different freelance (自由职业) comedians and celebrities each program, although the program is generally hosted by the same compere (主持人). Talk shows evolved in tandem (联合) with the Japanese variety show and it is very common for talk shows to borrow variety elements, typically by having celebrity guests attempt some kind of amusingly incongruous

(不协调的) activity. Often, one of the guests will be a foreign talent in order to provide comedy or to comment on matters related to Western culture. Comedic material is commonly written and rehearsed before tapings with or without a live audience.

Korean and Taiwanese talk shows have used the panel format similar to Japanese programs and rely on famous celebrities and comedic banter (玩笑) than topics. Their programs often shorten interviews from lengthy tapings.

In Brazil, Jô Soares inaugurated (开创) the genre with *Jô Soares Onze e Meia* (*Jô Soares Eleven Thirty*) from 1988 to 1999. In 2000, Soares took his show's format to *Rede Globo*, where it was then called *Programa do Jô*, and hosts the program until the present day.

I. Choose the best choice to answer or finish each of the following questions.

1. Which is NOT the content of breakfast chat?

    A. Celebrity interviews.   B. Musical performances.

    C. Psychological problems.   D. Political coverage.

2. Which of the following statements about late-night talk shows is true?

    A. It is about celebrity guests' work and lives.

    B. It is about some unusual or controversial topics.

    C. It is about news, politics, or popular culture.

    D. It is about entertainment and lifestyle.

3. _____ discusses topics of the plain weird.

    A. *The Best Damn Sports Show Period*   B. *Coast to Coast AM*

    C. *The Tonight Show*   D. *Car Talk*

4. _____ hosted the first television talk show.

    A. Art Bell   B. George Noory   C. Joe Franklin   D. Max Kellerman

5. _____ is the world's longest-running talk show.

    A. *The Late Late Show*   B. *The Baugh Experience*

    C. *Programa do Jô*   D. *The Tonight Show*

II. Match the words with their definitions.

WORDS	DEFINITIONS
1. episode	A. an entertainer who makes people laugh by telling jokes or funny stories
2. alternate	B. to send out programs on television or radio
3. controversial	C. one part of a story that is broadcast on television or radio in several parts
4. comedian	D. happening or following one after the other regularly
5. broadcast	E. causing a lot of angry public discussion and disagreement

III. Decide whether the following statements are true or false according to Passage III.

1. In many cases, the hosts become notable because of the talk show they host. (   )

2. Breakfast chat focuses on entertainment and lifestyle features. (   )

3. Late-night talk shows are often hosted by comedians and invite celebrity guests. (   )

4. *Space Ghost Coast to Coast* is a typical Sunday morning talk. (   )

5. Breakfast television has become popular in both Latin American and the United States. (   )

6. Besides politics, other subjects are also appeared in radio talk show. (   )

7. *The Tonight Show*, the longest-running talk show in the world has been on for over 60 years.
   (   )

8. The world record for the longest talk show was created by two Ukrainians in 2011. (   )

9. Talk shows in Japan have commonly borrowed some elements from variety show. (   )

10. Korean and Japanese talk shows share the similar format. (   )

Unit 8

Food

Lead-in

For some people food is just a necessity to satisfy basic needs, for the others, food is more than just a basic necessity, but a pleasure that plays a significant role in their understanding of happiness. There are so many different cuisines (菜肴) and food preferences built by cultural and ethnical (种族的) backgrounds, geographical (地理的) locations and social classes. Food can tell us a lot about the history and traditions of various nations and regions.

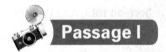

Why Buy Local Food?

Think Before Reading

1. Do you know what local food is?
2. Does your family often have local food?
3. Have you wondered why it's important to buy local food?

Local food is now a mainstream (主流) trend, with more and more people seeking out fresh, local options for produce and other foods. And more restaurants are sourcing (来源于) locally grown ingredients as well, often using the term farm-to-table.

But what is "local" food? How big of an impact does eating local food have on your health and the planet? And why is it important to know more about where your food comes from? There's no formal definition of the term local food. But one common definition of "local" food is food grown within 100 miles of its point of sale or consumption.

But it's up to you to decide what buying local food means to you. Maybe it means food grown and produced in your state or your region. Or maybe it means that it comes from farmers you know and can talk to — for example, at a farmer's market or through a CSA (加拿大标准协会). And for some people, "local" is more about the values of small-scale and community-based than about a specific geographic configuration (分布). More and more people want to know where their food comes from and the farming practices of the farmers that grow and produce it. And this is important for many reasons: It helps you develop a connection with food. You become more aware of what

you're putting in your body. You vote every time you shop, and with knowledge comes the ability to support food and growers you believe in.

Local food can be better for your health for a few reasons. To begin with, local foods often retain more nutrients. Local produce is allowed to ripen naturally, while food that travels long distances is often picked before it's ripe. And food picked fresh and in season doesn't have to travel far before being sold.

Choosing fruits and vegetables grown in season may also be healthier. When researchers at Montclair State University compared the vitamin C content of broccoli (西兰花) grown in season

with broccoli imported out of season, they found the latter had only half the vitamin C.

Another study published in the Journal of Agricultural and Food Chemistry found that the levels of health-promoting anthocyanin pigments (花青素) more than quadrupled (四倍) as blackberries became fully ripe.

In addition, locally grown produce may be safer. When they are imported and out of season, fruits like tomatoes, bananas, and pears are often picked unripe. And then, they are artificially "ripened" with ethylene gas (乙烯气体).

Also, foods from local growers may contain less (or no) pesticides (杀虫剂). Farmers have to pay an extra fee to become certified organic (经过有机认证的). Some small-scale farmers use organic methods but aren't certified because they simply aren't big enough to be able to afford the certification fees. Even if they aren't organic, small farmers tend to use fewer chemicals than large, industrialized farms.

If you can, talk to your farmers at your local market and ask them what (if any) pesticides they use. And be sure to wash your produce thoroughly to reduce your exposure to pesticides — which is especially important for pregnant women and children.

Food is one of the leading drivers of climate change. Eating more local food reduces CO_2 emissions (排放) by reducing food miles — the distance food travels from farm to consumer. The average piece of produce in the US travels 1,500 miles, while local food may only travel 100 miles

(or less), according to researcher Rich Pirog at the Leopold Center for Sustainable Agriculture at Iowa State University.

Local food helps preserve green space. When local farmers are well compensated (赔偿) for their products, they are less likely to sell their land to developers. Likewise, with growing consumer demand, young farmers are increasingly likely to enter the marketplace

by developing unused space, such as empty lots, into thriving urban gardens — many of which are grown organically.

Eating more local food can be one part of the solution. But, local is not the whole picture of food sustainability (可持续性). The impact our food choices have on the environment includes many factors.

In some cases, food produced farther away may be more sustainable if it's grown more responsibly, if it carries a smaller ecological (生态的) footprint, or if it's in season. Choosing more plant-based foods is an important part of the equation as well. If you want to eat a more sustainable diet, look for foods that are local, organic, and low on the food chain. The higher the percentage of your protein intake that comes from plant foods, the more earth-friendly and healthful your diet will be.

I. Match the words with their definitions.

WORDS	DEFINITIONS
1. local	A. stated explicitly or in detail
2. specific	B. of or belonging to or characteristic of a particular locality or neighborhood
3. retain	C. simple and healthful and close to nature
4. organic	D. hold back within
5. sustainability	E. capable of being sustained

II. Decide whether the following statements are true or false according to Passage I.

1. Some local vegetable contains more nutrients than imported one. (   )

2. All the local foods are organic. (   )

3. Having local foods can help to reduce air pollution. (   )

4. Local farms would grow on the unused field if they get more money for their products. (   )

5. Eating plant-based foods is less healthy than animal-based foods. (   )

III. Fill in the blanks in the following passage with words from Passage I.

Local foods are 1_____ nowadays all around the world. And more restaurants are offering local foods. They are usually grown around the 2_____ area. Having local foods is 3_____ for you and better for the 4_____. Local foods usually contain

more 5_____. If you want to eat a more sustainable diet, local foods are good choices. What's more, reducing food miles may help to reduce the emissions of CO_2.

Passage II

What Food Tells Us about Culture

Think Before Reading

1. Have you ever wondered what the food you eat everyday can tell you about where you come from?

2. Have you ever wondered why people from different parts of the world eat different types of food?

3. Do you ever ask yourself why certain foods or cooking traditions are so important to your culture?

People connect to their cultural or ethnic group through similar food patterns. Immigrants often use food as a means of keeping their cultural identity. People from different cultural backgrounds eat different foods. The ingredients (配料), methods of preparation, preservation (保存) techniques, and types of food eaten at different meals vary among cultures. The areas in which families live — and where their ancestors originated — influence food likes and dislikes. These food preferences result in patterns of food choices within a cultural or regional group.

Food items themselves have meaning attached to them. In many Western countries a box of chocolates would be viewed as a proper gift. The recipient of the gift would react differently to a gift of cabbage or carrots than to chocolate. In other countries chocolates might be a less appropriate gift.

Nations or countries are frequently associated with certain foods. For example, many people associate Italy with pizza and pasta (意大利面). Yet Italians eat many other foods, and types of pasta dishes vary throughout Italy. Methods of preparation and types of food vary by regions of a nation. Some families in the United States prefer to eat "meat and potatoes", but "meat and potatoes" are not eaten on a regular basis, nor even

preferred, by many in the United States and would not be labeled a national cuisine. Grits, a coarsely ground corn that is boiled, is eaten by families in the southern United States. A package of grits is only available in the largest supermarkets in the upper Midwest and would have been difficult to find even in large Midwestern supermarkets twenty years ago.

Regional food habits do exist, but they also change over time. As people immigrate, food practices and preferences are imported and exported. Families move to other locations, bringing their food preferences with them. They may cook their old dishes with new ingredients, or experiment with new dish, using new ingredients to match their own tastes. In addition, food itself is imported from other countries. Approximately 80 percent of Samoa's (南太平洋群岛国家萨摩亚) food requirements are imported from the United States, New Zealand, or Australia. Because people and food are mobile, attempts to characterize a country or people by what they eat are often different too.

Nevertheless, what is considered eatable in some parts of the world might be considered uneatable in other parts. Although food is often selected with some attention to physical need, the values or beliefs a society prefers to have potential food items define what families within a cultural group will eat. For example, both plant and animal sources may contribute to meeting nutritional requirements for protein (蛋白质); soybeans, beef, horsemeat, and dog meat are all adequate

protein sources. Yet, due to the symbolism attached to these protein sources, they are not equally available in all societies. Moreover, even when the foods perceived to be undesirable are available, they are not likely to be eaten by people who have a strong emotional reaction against the potential food item.

Some food beliefs and practices are due to religious beliefs. The dietary laws (饮食定律), which describe the

use and preparation of animal foods, are followed for purposes of spiritual health. Many followers of Buddhism, Hinduism, and Jainism are vegetarians, in part, because of a doctrine of non-injury or nonviolence.

In addition to influencing food choices, culture also plays a role in food-related etiquette (礼节). People in Western societies may refer to food-related etiquette as table manners, a phrase that tells the cultural expectation of eating food or meals at a table. Some people eat with forks and spoons; more people use fingers or chopsticks. However, utensil (工具) choice is much more complicated than choosing chopsticks, fingers, or flatware. Among some groups who primarily eat food with their fingers, diners use only the right hand to eat. Some people use only three fingers of the right hand. Among other groups, use of both hands is acceptable. In some countries, licking (舔) the fingers is polite; in others, licking the fingers is considered impolite. Rules regarding polite eating may increase in formal settings. At some formal dinners, a person might be expected to choose the "right" fork from among two or three choices to match the food being eaten at a certain point in the meal.

The amount people eat and leave uneaten also varies from group to group. Some people from Middle Eastern and Southeast Asian countries might leave a little bit of food on their plates in order to indicate that their hunger has been satisfied. Cooks from other locations might be offended if food is left on the plate, indicating that the guest may have disliked the food. Similarly, a clean plate might signify either satisfaction with the meal or desire for more food.

Even the role of conversation during mealtime varies from place to place. Many families believe that mealtime is a good time to converse and to "catch up" on the lives of family and friends. Among other families, conversation during a meal is acceptable, but the topics of conversation are limited. In some Southeast Asian countries it is considered polite to limit conversation during a meal.

Food traditions vary widely throughout the world. Even among people who share similar cultural backgrounds and some of the same food habits, eating patterns are not identical. Further, families vary from their own daily routines on holidays, when traveling, or when guests are present.

Men eat differently from women. People of different age groups eat differently. However, in most parts of the world, food is associated with hospitality (好客) and expression of friendship. Therefore, sensitivity (敏感) to food rules and customs is important in building and strengthening cross-cultural relationships.

I. Choose the best choice to answer or finish each of the following questions.

1. In some cultures, people would not eat dogs even though they are available because _____.

   A. dogs are attached to human emotions

   B. the taste of dog meat is not good

   C. it is forbidden by the local governments

   D. dogs are not good sources of protein

2. Which of the following factors is not mentioned to influence food choice according to the passage?

   A. Religious believes.　　　　　　B. Culture.

   C. Tradition.　　　　　　　　　　D. Color.

3. According to the passage, chocolate might be a more proper gift in _____.

   A. America　　　B. India　　　C. Egypt　　　D. China

4. Regional food habit may change according to _____.

   A. time and location　　　　　　B. mood and emotion

   C. climate and circumstance　　　D. tradition and custom

5. When people are at table in western countries, they prefer to follow _____.

   A. the habit of the hosts　　　　　B. the table manners

   C. their own preference　　　　　D. the guests' preferences

II. Match the words with their definitions.

WORDS	DEFINITIONS
1. associate	A. the feeling that accompanies an experience of failures
2. frustration	B. be the cause or source of
3. identity	C. the act of making something different
4. alteration	D. name and personal details
5. yield	E. make a logical or causal connection

III. Decide whether the following statements are true or false according to Passage II.

1. "Meat and potatoes" is labeled as a national dish in USA. (   )

2. Leftovers are regarded as proper in Southeast Asia. (   )

3. All the followers of Buddhism are vegetarians. (   )

4. A food habit may change with circumstances. (   )

5. Any topic during a meal is encouraged in Southeast Asian Countries. (   )

Cultural Differences in Body Language to Be Aware of

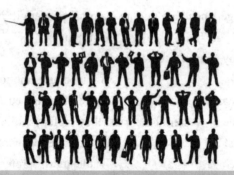

Think Before Reading

1. What is body language?

2. Have you realized that there are different ody languages in different cultures?

3. What is the proper way to use our body language in a cross-cultural communication?

Body language makes up the largest part of our non-verbal communication — eye contact, gestures, and facial expressions and can convey powerful messages. As William Shakespeare said in *Troilus and Cressida* (《皆大欢喜》) — "There's language in her eye, her cheek, her lip". However, there are substantial (大量的) cultural differences in how people use body language to communicate. Sometimes it is very obvious, many times very subtle (微妙的). Whether in a culturally diverse company or visiting emerging markets, understanding what people mean through their body language can be a challenge.

Greetings with a Handshake

Even the simple handshake can vary from culture to culture. A handshake is widely accepted as the norm; however you'll need to vary the firmness depending on the location. Western culture typically perceives a strong handshake as authoritative and confidence, where as many parts of the Far East perceive a strong handshake as aggressive, and usually bow instead. In parts of Northern Europe, a quick firm handshake is the norm. In parts of Southern Europe, Central and South America, a handshake is longer and warmer, with the left hand usually touching the clasped (握紧的) hands or elbow. Beware that in Turkey, a firm handshake is considered rude and aggressive. In certain African countries, a limp (无力地) handshake is the standard. Men in Islamic countries never shake the hands of women outside the family.

Facial Expressions

Many facial expressions appear to be universal and recognized all over the globe. Research carried out by the Paul Ekman Group, an American psychologist, showed that over 90% of common facial expressions were identified by people in very different cultures. Over 10,000 facial expressions were created for the study and shown to different western cultures and isolated, pre-literate (没有文字的) African groups.

Hand Gestures

We use gestures as a way to emphasize points and illustrate what we are saying. Hand gestures can mean very different things in different cultures; the "OK" sign in Greece, Spain or Brazil means you are cursing somebody. In Turkey, it's meant to be an insult towards gay people. A thumb up in America and European cultures is an indicator of a job well done, however in Greece or the Middle East, it can mean "up yours".

Curling (弯曲) the index finger with the palm facing up is a common gesture that people in United States and parts of Europe use to beckon (召唤) someone to come closer. However, it is considered rude in China, East Asia, Malaysia, Singapore, the Philippines, and many other parts of the world. It's also considered extremely impolite to use this gesture with people. It is used only to beckon dogs in many Asian countries — and using it in the Philippines can get you arrested.

On Inauguration (就职) Day 2005, President George W. Bush raised his fist, with the index and little finger extended, in the shape of the Texas Longhorn football team logo. Newspapers around the world expressed their astonishment at the use of such a gesture. In many Mediterranean and Latin countries, such as Argentina, Brazil, Colombia, Cuba, Spain, Italy and Portugal, to make this sign at someone is to tell them that their spouse (配偶) is cheating on them.

Eye Contact

In most western countries, eye contact is a sign of confidence and attentiveness. We tend to assume that if someone looks away while we are talking to them, they're disinterested and looking for someone else to talk to. In many Middle Eastern countries, same-gender eye contact tends to be more sustained and intense than the western standard. In some of these countries, eye contact beyond a brief glance between the sexes is deemed inappropriate.

In many Asian, African, and Latin American countries, however, this unbroken eye contact would be considered aggressive and confrontational (对抗的). These cultures tend to be quite conscious of hierarchy (等级制度), and avoiding eye contact is a sign of respect for bosses and elders. In these parts of the world, children won't look at an adult who is speaking to them, and nor will employees to their bosses.

Moving Your Head

In some parts of India, people tilt (倾斜) their head from side to side to confirm something and demonstrate that they are actively listening. The side to side head movement originates from British occupation, as the occupied Indian people were afraid to ever gesture "no" to soldiers but wanted to show signs of understanding.

Touch

Northern Europe and the Far East are classed as non-contact cultures. There is very little physical contact beyond a handshake with people we don't know well. Even accidentally brushing someone's arm on the street warrants (有理由要求) an apology. An innocent hug  made headlines around the world in 2009 when America's first lady, Michelle Obama, broke royal protocol (皇家礼仪) on a visit to Britain by hugging the Queen. By comparison, in the high-contact cultures of the Middle East, Latin America, and southern Europe, physical touch is a big part of socializing.

In much of the Arab world, men hold hands and kiss each other in greeting, but would never do the same with a woman. In Thailand and Laos, it is taboo to touch anyone's head, even children. In South Korea, elders can touch younger people with force when trying to get through a crowd, but younger people can't do the same.

High Contact cultures tend to stand close when speaking and make physical contact more often. Latin America, southern Europe and most Middle Eastern nations are examples. Medium Contact cultures stand quite close when speaking and will touch on occasion. Such cultures include Northern Europe and North America. Low Contact cultures stand at a greater distance and generally avoid physical contact. The Far East is an example. These rules are usually quite complex. They  may differ depending on the age, gender, ethnicity, profession and status of the people involved.

Sitting Positions

Be aware of your posture when you attend meetings or are dining. Sitting cross-legged is seen as disrespectful in Japan, especially in the presence of someone older or more respected than you. Showing the soles (鞋底) of your shoes or feet can offend people in parts of the Middle East and India. That is why throwing shoes at someone is a form of protest and an insult in many parts of the world — as former US President George W. Bush famously discovered on a visit to Iraq in 2008.

Silence

Though it can feel like a void (空隙) in communication, silence can be very meaningful in different cultural contexts. Western cultures, especially North America and the UK, tend to view silence as problematic. In our interactions at work, school, or with friends, silence is uncomfortable. It is often perceived as a sign of inattentiveness or disinterest.

In other cultures, however, silence is not viewed as a negative circumstance. In China, silence can be used to show agreement and receptiveness. In many aboriginal (原始的) cultures, a question will be answered only after a period of contemplative (沉思的) silence. In Japan, silence from women can be considered an expression of femininity (女性特质).

Gender

In many cultures, what is acceptable for a man may not be acceptable for a woman. The most obvious example is the issue of covering your head in some Muslim countries, but also, within religions such as Islam and Hinduism, shaking a woman's hand can be considered offensive.

Conclusion

Modern transportation and an increase in expendable income allow us to visit a huge range of cultures. We've discussed how gestures, eye contact, greetings and physical contact can have very different meanings in different countries and cultures so you'll want to learn as much as you can about the country's etiquette (礼仪), values and styles of communication before you visit. Being able to understand cultural differences will improve your working relationships and potentially make you more successful in an increasingly globalized, multi-cultural working world.

I. Choose the best choice to answer or finish each of the following questions.

1. In this passage, the author is trying to _____ in cross cultural communications.

   A. remind people to be aware of their dressings

   B. teach the reader proper ways of behaviors

   C. show us the cultural differences in the world

   D. suggest us to speak politely

2. According to the passage, in which of the following situations is body language important?

   A. In a single-cultural company.   B. In a newly-built supermarket.

   C. In a backward country.   D. In a multi-cultural corporation.

3. A firm hand shake is not proper in _____.

   A. America   B. Germany   C. Turkey   D. Brazil

4. President George W. Bush was misunderstood on his Inauguration Day in 2005 because

   _____.

   A. he made a wrong gesture   B. he arrested some Philippines

   C. he cheated his wife   D. he said some dirty words

5. If a man keeps looking at another man in the eyes in many Middle Eastern countries, it

   is _____.

   A. unacceptable   B. acceptable   C. unclear   D. questionable

II. Match the words with their definitions.

WORDS	DEFINITIONS
1. convey	A. the act of making a strong public expression of disagreement and disapproval
2. identify	B. a ban resulting from social custom or emotional aversion
3. occupy	C. march aggressively into another's territory by military force for the purposes of conquest
4. taboo	D. recognize as being
5. protest	E. make known; pass on information

III. Decide whether the following statements are true or false according to Passage III.

1. If a clerk looks into the eyes of his leader in many Asian countries, it is regarded as being impolite. (   )

2. In some parts of India, people move their head from side to side to express their disagreement. (   )

3. According to the British royal protocol, nobody can hug the Queen. (   )

4. Throwing shoes at someone is a form of protest and an insult in parts of the Middle East and India. (   )

5. Silence in communication is more acceptable in the western culture than it is in the Chinese culture. (   )